PAUL STENHOUSE

A Distinctive and Distinguished Missionary of the Sacred Heart

PAUL STENHOUSE

*A Distinctive
and Distinguished
Missionary of the
Sacred Heart*

Edited by
Peter Malone MSC

AUSTRALIAN SCHOLARLY

First published 2020 by
Australian Scholarly Publishing Pty Ltd

Australian Scholarly Publishing Pty Ltd
7 Lt Lothian St Nth, North Melbourne, Vic 3051
enquiry@scholarly.info / www.scholarly.info

ISBN 978-1-922454-03-4

Cover design: Wayne Saunders

CONTENTS

MINISTRY

TRIBUTES

FOREWORD

Central to Paul Stenhouses's life was Jesus.

My name is Chris McPhee, I am a Missionary of the Sacred Heart and, at present the Provincial of the Australian Province.

I met Paul, really for the first time in Rome when I was there as Assistant General (2011–17). Prior to this, was when I was doing my theological studies at St Paul's National Seminary, Kensington, back in 1996 and there Paul gave us a week on the Samaritans.

It was always great when Paul came to Rome. For one, he was a fellow Aussie and two, he was my brother MSC. Anyway, after dinner, he and I would find ourselves alone in the loungeroom discussing all the big issues of the world, religious life and of the Church. As you can imagine, as the night wore on, so too did our discussions. On many occasions, I would find myself being questioned on a number of theological points. But whatever our differences, there was always one central point that we agreed on—Jesus—and to this we never had a disagreement. You see, for me, Paul was a Missionary of the Sacred Heart through and through and through.

As Michael Fallon MSC, states in his Eulogy; 'It was from his faith in God as revealed in the heart of Jesus that Paul got his inspiration.' As I witnessed to Paul's life and have read through this book, indeed, 'Paul's heart was as big as the world.' How true!

Paul had a big picture—a broad paint brush of the world

and of all the things that were important and that mattered. As you read through this book, you'll see what an extraordinary man Paul was, as well as, a very ordinary down to earth human being.

For many, the remembering will be about his personal relationships. For others, it will be about his defence of the Church—Catholic. For others, his understanding and insights about Islam, and then for others, his love of literature, poetry and the fine arts, and then again for others, his love of action films and McDonalds.

In all this, everything he did, everything he read, wrote and authored, was always through the lens of being a Missionary of the Sacred Heart.

Coming back to those evenings in Rome, Paul, to me, was a man who was relational. He could listen, take time out, share, discuss and converse with all people. As you will see from those who have written in this book, whether they be some of this country's top academics, judges, politicians, cardinals, bishops, or just very ordinary human beings like you and me, Paul always had time for people.

As Anthony Brereton says in his article, 'I often visited Paul for a chat, and he was always kind, helpful and interested in talking about learning, pedagogy and faith.'

Central to Paul's working life and ministry was the *Annals* and as John Madden in his article states; 'After God, the Catholic Church was Paul's greatest love.'

In the many discussions I had with Paul, both here and in Rome, I always got the image that Paul saw the Church as the Body of Christ, and to him, being a missionary of the Heart of Christ, it was up to him, through the *Annals*, to defend the

Church at all costs. Again, from John Madden's article. 'If people would only take time to get to know the Church, they could not help falling in love with her.'

In many ways, Paul saw the *Annals* as a way to help mould our future world, to promote a love for what is true, good and beautiful. For me, through this medium, Paul was convincing with his insights, his knowledge, his scriptural understandings, his cultural sensitivities, and his wisdom about critiquing the present moment. In a way, he gave meaning, direction, and a way through this modern world we live in.

In his book 'Islam; Context and Complexity' Paul writes that the greater part of his academic life was not a study of Islam, but a study of Arabic and Hebrew literature of the Samaritans. Through this academic study and research, it finally led him into the world of Islam. As Piers Paul Reid states here; 'Above all, he [Paul] laments the lack of clear riposte to Islamism. Piers Paul Read goes on to say that 'he [Paul] concurs with the Italian Senator Marcello Pera that the fibre of the West is permeated by a mixture of timidity, prudence, convenience, reluctance and fear.'

But in all this academia, Paul was a very personal, relational, and pastoral human being. His work with the Asian Catholic Community here in Sydney is testament to this. As one family remembered; 'Fr Paul Stenhouse to us meant '101 Solutions'. He was here with our family since the very day we set foot in Australia.' In all, 'Father Paul was a foster father, career advisor, confidant, discussions partner, tour guide, a big and warm-hearted priest to us.'

Which brings me back to the title of this book—which rightly says; 'A Distinctive and Distinguished Missionary of the Sacred Heart.'

It gives me great pleasure to recommend to people of all stages of life, faith, political persuasion, theological and historical bent to read this book as a testament to an ordinary human being who did extraordinary things with his life.

As I began this Foreword, I will also finish it with the fact that for Paul, his life was one that continually pointed to the truth, to meaning, to the value of human life, to the Sacred, and for him it was all summed up in living as one of many Missionaries of the Sacred Heart of Jesus.

Enjoy!

Chris R McPhee MSC
Provincial MSC Australia
Treand House, Coogee, NSW
Sunday, 19 July 2020

PART I

PAUL STENHOUSE, MSC

Eulogy For Paul

Michael Fallon MSC

Our Lady of the Rosary Church, Requiem Mass,
Wednesday 27th November 2019.
'Man goes forth to his work and to his labour
until the evening' (Psalm 104:23).

The early years

Our very dear friend Paul Francis Lester Stenhouse was born
on December 9, 1935. Paul's father, Richard, was born in New
Zealand and met and married Paul's mother, May Kathleen
Huntley Skinner in Camden, NSW. This was the time of the
Depression. At the time of Paul's birth, his father had found
work in Casino. Unfortunately, his father died, and so Paul
and Richard, his elder brother by 18 months, never had the
chance to know him. Mrs Stenhouse brought the boys up

in a house in Oxley Street Camden where her mother and two uncles lived. It was close to the home of her childhood, Matavai, in Cobbitty.

Paul's primary schooling was partly home-schooling by his mother and partly with the Sisters of Saint Joseph at Saint Paul's Convent. Paul's mother was raised in the Anglican Church and she had and maintained many close acquaintances and friends in that community. However, in 1924 when she was in her 21st year, she read herself into the Catholic Church.

A mother's profound influence

Her influence on Paul was immense. Among other things she gave Paul a love for books. French fairy tales were on the menu from the start. Paul had an amazing aptitude for languages. He picked up from his mother a deep respect for people, whatever their religious upbringing, along with an unshakable conviction of the place of the Catholic Church in Christianity. The word 'Catholic' says it all. It means all-embracing. To quote something Paul wrote: 'There is nothing limited about our Faith. We should be universal in our belief; in our acceptance of others, in our appreciation of the total picture. Partial reality, like partial truth, should be distasteful to us. We belong to the most culturally and linguistically diversified community in the world. We are heirs to traditions which, if properly understood, would enrich not just our own lives, but the lives of all our fellow-citizens.'

Training in journalism

Paul's first job, aged 14, was with *The Camden News*. In 1953 this young 17-year-old would-be linotypist/compositor/reporter saw an advertisement in the *Annals*, a magazine published by the Missionaries of the Sacred Heart, inviting boys interested in becoming priests to come to St Mary's Towers Douglas Park, which in those days was a boarding school, and only 20 minutes from Camden. Paul applied and was accepted into the Intermediate class. His quick intelligence enabled him to catch up on the formal education he was not able to pursue as a boy.

His connection with the *Annals* was to prove providential. At the completion of his novitiate Paul took vows on February 26 1957. He then did his priestly studies in the monastery at Croydon Victoria and was ordained a priest in Sydney on July 20, 1963. The following year 1964 he was appointed Business Manager of *Annals*, and Editor two years later, thus beginning a career with the magazine that, apart from a four-year absence as personal secretary to the MSC General in Rome, he has faithfully carried out right up to his death. In its heyday, the *Annals* had a circulation greater than the *Bulletin*, the leading news magazine of the day, and in the publishing world, the Annals was considered an extraordinary phenomenon.

Semitic studies

In 1973 Paul received a BA (Hons) from the University of Sydney majoring in Samaritan Studies and Arabic. He produced a critical edition and translation of the historical sections of the Samaritan Hebrew Hilukh, a purity code. In 1982 he received a PhD from the University of Sydney for his Critical Edition of the Middle Arabic Text of the Samaritan Chronicle of Abu 'l-Fath. It is worth noting that before Paul could produce a commentary on the text, he had to translate it, and before he could translate he had to rediscover the dictionary and grammar for medieval Samaritan. As a result Paul's PhD is three volumes, and took years to be examined, because he was the only person who knew this area in detail.

Paul was a foundation member of the Council of the *Société d'Études Samaritaines* within the Collège de France, Paris. He has delivered papers at Colloquia organised by the Société, held in Paris, Tel Aviv and Jerusalem, Oxford, Venice, Helsinki, Budapest, Zurich and Tartu, Estonia. Paul wrote the article on 'Samaritans' for the *Encyclopaedia of the Qur'ān*, June 2002.

Paul was awarded an honorary doctorate by the University of Notre Dame, and also by the Catholic University. Paul has written and lectured extensively on Middle Eastern Politics and history. His special interest over the past 40 years has been Lebanon/Syria, and the Balkans.

In 1988 he received an MA (Hons) from the University of New England for a Literary Biography of John Farrell, Paul's great-grandfather, a 19th Century Australian journalist and reformer. Scholarly Press Melbourne published Paul's book on John Farrell last year, and his book on *Islam, context and complexity* this year. Paul worked generously and untiringly right to the end.

'His intellect was amazing'

We thank God for the gift we have shared in knowing Paul. His intellect was amazing. His commitment to pursue truth, and to share what he discovered so honestly and thoroughly over the past 56 years since his ordination have been awe-inspiring. His respect for those who formed judgments that differed from his was admirable, but I don't think it is too strong to say that he hated the all-pervasive laziness that claims that there is no such thing as truth, and that one opinion is as good as another. We may not agree with everything Paul said or wrote, but we have to admire his research displayed in the thoroughness in which he footnoted every statement.

I could go on forever speaking of his amazing mind. But he did have an even greater gift: his heart. I don't know a hundredth of it, and I am sure everyone here this morning would have many stories to tell. I don't know of anyone who experienced need and turned to Paul who did not experience his loving, practical and committed care. One example, which perhaps some of you had first hand experience of, was his care for international students, and migrants more generally. Paul would meet people at the airport, deliver them to appointments, find them accommodation, accompany them to immigration tribunals, badger university administrations — and any academic who he thought could help — on their behalf. He also took on the role of reassuring anxious parents, worried about their children overseas. And finally, of course, he could marry them and baptise their children. Paul was, indeed, a Missionary of the Sacred Heart of Jesus.

The Sacred Heart of Jesus

It was from his faith in God as revealed in the heart of Jesus that Paul got his inspiration. I can hear Paul in something John Henry Newman, recently canonised wrote: 'I do not care to overcome people's reason without touching their hearts' (*A Grammar of Assent*). Paul's heart was as big as the world. In 1997 he was appointed Chairman of the Australian Office of the world-wide organization *Aid to the Church in Need*. We can appreciate Paul's mind. It may not have been as apparent that his mind was guided, in ways that Paul himself may not have realised, by his sensitive heart. He agonised even to think that he might hurt someone or let someone down.

In regard to the deep friendships Paul made I would like to quote from Winston Churchill's eulogy (November 12, 1940) to Neville Chamberlain: 'History with its flickering lamp stumbles along the trail of the past, trying to reconstruct its scenes, to revive its echoes, and to kindle with pale gleams the passions of former days'. Having known and been close to Paul since we first met at Saint Mary's Towers in 1953, I have some idea of what Churchill meant.

I would like now to quote from Pope Francis's reflection at the close of the Year of Mercy: 'Our life with its joys and sorrows is something unique and unrepeatable, that takes place under the merciful gaze of God. This demands, especially of priests, a careful, far-sighted spiritual discernment, so that everyone, none excluded, can feel accepted by God, participate actively in the community and be part of the People of God which journeys tirelessly towards the fullness of God's kingdom of justice, love, forgiveness and mercy.' Thank you, Paul, for showing this to us.

I conclude by returning to the *Annals* and giving the final word to dear Paul who writes in the final edition of the *Annals*, completed only a few days ago. I quote: 'In a poem of Dame Mary Gilmore's "By the Roadside", printed for the first time in *Annals* (December, 1926), we can find a crystallising of the aims of this most Australian of Catholic Magazines.' Paul then quotes from the poem: 'Wonder is dead, you say! / Wonder can never die / Not while within a shining pool / A man can see the sky.' Paul goes on: 'It is as a shining pool reflecting the wonders of God and God's creation that *Annals* should be remembered. Age could do little to mar the image that it reflects.' It is somehow fitting that after almost 50 years as editor of *Annals* Paul managed to contribute to and edit the final edition of the magazine as he was dying.

At the Last Supper Jesus prayed: 'Father, I want those you have given me to be with me where I am … May the love with which you loved me be with them, so that I too may be with them.' Paul, you have known this love, and you have revealed it to us. Till we meet again dear friend in the mystery of God's love, we bid you farewell and thank you for the gift and inspiration you have been to us all. Thank you for your love.

Random Memories

Paul Stenhouse

My memories of growing up in Camden from the late 1930s until 1953 are, on the whole, happy ones. For a while I seem to spend a long time bed-ridden as I had various illnesses that stopped my getting what you could call a normal schooling, gave me a unique opportunity to be educated by my mother. I am a product of home schooling more than anything else.

My mother had been taught by Mr Chittick in the old Cobbity public school and later on by Canon Allnut at the Rectory in Cobbity. She loved history and poetry and used to read French fairytales to me and Richard from old volumes of *Contes et Legendes* which may still be around somewhere. I loved them, and like all children exposed to languages early, I took to French like a duck to water. It's still my favourite foreign language though Italian is a close second.

All the things that are said these days about the advantages of children being read to by parents and siblings are true from my experience. Picture books are more valuable than TV. And being read to is a wonderful aid to bonding between adults and children. I loved being read to. My mother and grandmother and my brother Richard would read to me until they discovered that I knew perfectly well how to read, and was exploiting their kind natures.

Neither Richard nor I had many toys—we couldn't afford them. Mostly such presents as we received on birthdays or

Christmas would be books. I'm ashamed when I recall a terrible tantrum I put on when yet another book was given for my birthday or at Christmas.

Richard and I lived in a house in Oxley Street with my grandmother and mother, my uncles Frank and Roy, and two guests—Bessie O'Dwyer and a tall refined old gentleman who kept to himself and whose name escapes me. These had come with us to the old rambling timber house in Oxley Street from the Coaching Inn in Argyle Street close to the Royal Hotel. Before it was bought by my grandmother and mother and paid for by Richard and me when we went to work, the Oxley Street house had belonged to Tamar Watson. It had been built by her father sometime in the previous century. Tamar was the wife of Anglican bishop Edward Wilton, the Rector of Cobbity when we were children, and was often to be seen driving the Bishop around the district in their little Morris Minor, or was it a Ford Anglia?

Bessie claimed to hear the wailing of the Banshee whenever someone was about to die. That was enough to give Richard and me plenty to think about whenever Bessie appeared on the verandah, to sit with my grandmother. When Bessie died, we wondered if she heard the Banshee. We couldn't ever recall ever hearing it—no we listened hard enough.

My first memory in Camden is of the beautiful old Coaching Inn in Argyle Street where we lived with our grandmother. It has long since disappeared, like Matavai—my mother's old house at Cobbity, just up from our cousins, the Holtzs, at Marshdale—before either could be saved by some Government department interested in preserving vestiges of Australia's remote past.

Matavai's new owners built a modern bungalow in place of the old lathes and plaster convict-brick homestead with its upstairs ballroom for dancing on Harvest Festivals, and our great-grandmother's side-saddle slung over one of the rafters. The Coaching Inn was demolished to make room for timber-jinkers and large machinery to enter the yard at the back,

There were large paving stones on the front verandah of the Coaching Inn, and in my mind's eye I can still see Richard walking past me wearing a brightly coloured cap as I sat on a high chair—I guess I was about 18 months old—and I reached out to grab his cap. He hung on to it, and so something had to give. I did. I fell onto the stones. He tells me he recalls that day vividly too.

Our great-great-great-grandfather Thomas Huntley, a farmer from Tenterden in Kent, was born in 1777, not long after Cook discovered Australia. His son, our great-great-grandfather George Huntley, was born in 1815 and came to Australia aged 24 on September 9, 1839 on the Cornwall. He married Eliza Willis from Crookwell in 1843.

The story of his family is acquiring Matavie at Cobbity, and our connection with the Latteys, Vicarys, Watsons, Stapleton's, Gregory's, Chappells, Holzs and Ahrenfelds and other local families has been touched on by my mother in her memories of growing up at Matavai.

When young George left England, he was called George Huntley—when he reached Sydney he had changed his name to George Huntley Skinner. That he was a remittance man is clear—as my mother's grandmother would tell stories about the funds drying up when her grandfather died. All his children carried the name Huntley and it has continued almost to this day.

Returning to the eight of us who lived in Oxley Street: from time to time our numbers number would increase. Tramps would come to Camden from Cobbity and stay with us. They had been accustomed to hospitality in Cobbity at Matavai, where my grandmother would never turn them away. So they continued to stay with us when the family moved to Camden. They lived in the house, ate with us and used the time to get their few clothes cleaned and ironed and then would set out again on their travels. They were proud men and would always find some work to do around the house while they were with us.

One such was George Blandford. He had become a Jehovah's Witness somewhere on his travels, and he pestered us boys about our being Catholic, but carefully avoided arguing with our mother. He had a beautiful voice, and Richard tells me that he got into the finals of the Amateur Hour on a few occasions.

Over the years I've been many times to London, and sometimes I stayed at St James's Church, Spanish Place—between Baker Street and Oxford Street. Actually the presbytery where I stayed is in George Street, parallel to Blandford Street. In the light of my own mother's ancestor's name change, I wondered what George's real name was. Or am I being unnecessarily suspicious? It could be a coincidence. But George was a Londoner and he never spoke of his past—at least not to us children.

My memories of Camden are of summer days, unvaryingly, and often unbearably, hot. Some relief was to be had by swimming in the Nepean river and sometimes when Richard and I were lucky enough we would be given the job of hauling huge (to us youngsters) blocks of ice back home from the ice works just up from the railway station. We had an icebox, no refrigerator, and at night I would read voraciously by hurricane lamp. This reading by lamp-light may have it affected my eyesight which seems always to have been poor.

The black frost of winter too burnt intelligibly on my memory. I thought I would never feel such cold as I did in those early years in Camden, until I found myself having living in Slovenia and Croatia in wintertime during the Tito era with snow piled up by the roadside, and ice on the streets, in temperatures many degrees below zero.

As for wind—however fiercely coldly the August winds blew in Camden when we were children, they were like gentle zephyrs compared to the indescribably bitter *Mistral* blowing from the Alps down the *Couloir de Rhone* at Château Combert outside Marseille, where I used to spend time in the middle 70s and early 80s. I was staying there when Pope John Paul I died, and Pope John Paul II was elected. How the poor farm workers could pick olives in January clinging precariously to ladders in the rapier-sharp wind, with their hands covered in festering chilblains, I'll never know.

Flood seemed to be a fairly regular occurrence in my childhood. Homes a little further down the street from us— the Watsons especially, and the Vicarys—suffered regularly and terribly from the inundations. On occasion we had floodwaters right under the floorboards of our home. The police tried to move us on—a futile hope, as anyone who knows my mother's stubbornness and my mother's Faith, would agree. Even if the houses closer to the river were underwater, she would never accept the fact that we would be flooded. Nor were we. Sometimes the top of the stalls of the horses at the Showground would be covered with water: and still we stood firm.

My mother wasn't one to give in to mere floodwater. On one occasion, I saw her stare down a charging cow, with head and horns lowered threateningly. She never flinched, and the cow veered away. I think a few people around the town would have thought the cow was foolish to try.

The Sisters of St Joseph taught me a lot, especially about generosity and self-sacrifice, and the sight of Mrs Burnell walking past St Paul's Convent School up John Street to do her shopping held out visions of freedom to a young boy who, curiously, never really enjoyed being in a proper school. Father O'Dea and his cousin, Miss O'Connor, who was his housekeeper—the people of Cobbity, Burragorang Valley, the Oaks, Menangle, Teresa Park—all form part of these memories.

Old Mrs Carlon from Burragorang kept us little children entranced with tales of hidden caves in the Valley, bigger and better than those named after the bushranger J.F. Nolan in the Blue Mountains. How I longed to get down to Burragorang on my own and explore them. A futile hope then, and certainly now, since the Warragamba Dam was built and Burragorang flooded. I recall feeling sad at what seemed the inadequate compensation paid to the pioneering families of Yerranderie and Burragorang who lost their homes and properties to the dam. Rumour had it that they got the pre-war value. Our Paradise Lost—and almost certainly undervalued.

Camden has changed so much now, even though to a superficial line much may appear to be the same. We had two cinemas—the old *Empire* on the corner of Argyle and Oxley Street which had been turned into a dance hall with a billiard room up top, and the other, the *Paramount* opposite the tram/train station in Elizabeth Street. Both belonged to Mr and Mrs Jackie Fox who lived somewhere in Hill Street. Was the name originally Fuchs? I thought so as a child, though I can't be sure.

Certainly the family names of some of our cousins suffered orthographic changes with the passing of time: Holtz became Holtz and Ahrenfeldt became Ahrenfeld. I was surprised to learn from an old Scottish lady who was housekeeper to the Parish Priest of Kiama in the early 60s that the Stenhouses, who belong to the clan Bruce, were the bodyguards of the early Scottish kings, and that our name should be pronounced *Stannish*. I can't see our pulling that off.

The train was technically a tram as there was no fence up between it and the road to Campbelltown. Along with the ice-works, the sawmill and the milk-works, it had gone the way of the paddocks where the swimming pool is now. Does Bruce Ferguson still have the nursery down from the old Carrington Hospital, I wonder.

Are the Chisholms, Rapleys, Channells, Stones, and Izzards still in Camden? What about the Heises and Hyneses, the Sidmans, Felds and Bruchhausers, the Thurns, Rheinbergers, Downes and Jefferises?

I owe my good health to the two doctors Jefferis and especially Dr Robert, who used to come home every day to see how I was, for months on end. Dr Croxton took out my tonsils, and Mr Hennings gave me my first watch. Dr Newton-Tabrett fitted me for my first glasses when I was about four years old, and the painful headaches I used to have ceased miraculously.

Do the Britwilltons in the Clark still own chemist shops here? Mr Butler who owned a bike shop in Argyle Street encouraged Richard to become a bike rider and gave him a beautiful racing bike with 'conloys and singles'—evocative words to describe magical lightweight tires made of what seemed like bamboo, and special glue-on tubes. Richard was at one time New South Wales Junior Country bike-riding champion. I was very proud of him, but never got accustomed to his riding at night up Razorback in winter to keep in trim.

I have fond memories of Mr George Sidman, who gave me my first job, on the *Camden News,* and taught me much. His brother Robert came from Campbelltown most days to work. A fine typographer, Bob, as we called him behind his back, had been gassed during WWI and was ailing. He believed in keeping young printers devils well occupied and was sparing in his praise. He impressed this 14-year-old with his ability to have a cat-nap on the benches of the printing office at lunchtime, and was no slouch at setting or 'dissing' type.

Mr George Sidman gave me a little book that I still treasure, entitled *The Law of Libel and the Press*, along with advice about writing that still stands me in good stead—especially about never writing down all that one knows. 'Keep something in reserve', he would say, 'you never know when it will be needed'.

I have fond memories, too, of Miss Llewela Davies (who worked in the front office of the *Camden News*) and her parents—all of them now gone to God—who encouraged and showed kindness to what must have seemed to them to be a very idiosyncratic child. This Davies father's Christian name was Christmas, not uncommon among Welshmen I understand, but it puzzled me mightily. Yet Noel didn't. The Manager of the *Camden News* was Mr Noel Behan. It's curious how a French name could sound right to a young Australian's ear, when a good old British name sounded out of place.

A person who took me under his journalistic wing in those very early years in Camden and to whom I look back with gratitude was Mr Gordon Thomas who reported Camden Council Meetings in the *Campbelltown News,* and on numerous occasions steered me safely around hidden and dangerous journalistic reefs. Gordon had a goatee beard, rare in those days of bewhiskered men, and had vast experience in newspaper work. He was a Canadian who had been on the Klondike, and ridden the rails during the Great Depression. Gordon settled in one of the then run-down yet beautiful old Colonial houses not far from Fisher's Ghost Bridge in the main street of Campbelltown. He died within a year or so of my leaving for Douglas Park aged 17, in July 1953.

Mr George Sidman died not long after he had retired. He sold the *Camden News* and the *Campbelltown News* to Mr Sid Richardson from Picton. I seem to recall his telling me that the Sidman's had a printer in Paris in the late 18th century until was confiscated by the Republicans and its lead type melted down to make bullets during the French Revolution.

All the men who were old to my young eyes seemed to have long beards. The older women carried parasols and wore broad-brimmed black hats. They also wore black or darkish veils, with mysterious dots on them that I thought looked like flies.

Most of my great-aunts and great-uncles kept peacocks on their farms. They were a feature of Marshdale which belonged to our cousins the Holzs and was next door to Matavai—as were the deliciously-strongly scented Muscatel grapes that seemed to be *de rigueur* around most farmhouses in those days, along with the mandatory chaff-cutter near the kitchen door. Aunty Mary Vicary on Cawdor Road always kept peacocks never house.

The old saddlery opposite Oxley Street in Argyle Street must be long gone. The narrow, two-story building next to or close to (I can't remember which) Furner's Hardware store, was always closed in my time. We thought that the Mrs Stevens (I hope I've remembered their name correctly) lived above it after their brother died, though I don't believe I ever saw them. The shop window in Argyle Street still had some saddles and bridles in it—and maybe some stirrups covered in dust. My cousin Geoff McAleer's father, Hubie, used to say a with a smile that Mr Stevens once made a saddle for someone and couldn't remember whom he sent it to.

I remember Hubie's dad whom we called grandfather McAleer, well. He used to sit in a rocking chair on the verandah of his house in Menangle and presided over family affairs like Charlton Heston just down from the Mountain top with the Ten Commandments—at least in this child's eyes. He was a prophetic figure with a long flowing beard, and he probably wasn't all that old.

The roads and paths then were populated mainly by horses and sulkies, and if there were cars, they were those exquisite, humanly manageable ones with headlights like eyes set on stalks, and with leather hoods that were retractable, dickie seats for exciting trips to the coast on the occasional Sundays in summer, and running boards ideal for picnics by the river at Cobbity. I remember our mother frightening us children when she almost choked on a piece of grass—a paspalum seed, I think—which the wind blew onto a sandwich she was eating one summer's evening by the river at the Grove. Fortunately for all our sakes she coughed up the offending seed.

I learned to swim by being tossed into the Nepean at Cobbity Bridge by my uncle Amos just before he went to the war. Fortunately he pulled his terrified nephew out—I was around four—before I drowned. To this day I can see the mussels in the sand at the bottom of the stream in what was then sparklingly clear and pure water

* * *

A final thought: I once visited Tenterden in Kent—associated with the Cinque Ports—where Huntleys, my mother's ancestors, came from. Around there one can still hear names like Huntley, Newton (my grandmother's sister Lucy Stapleton married a Newnham) Haffenden, Dengate, Tapley and (if I recall correctly) Clifton and Furner. So I wondered if there was some early link between Camden and Tenterden that might repay examination by someone interested in the very groups that have nourished the genetic tree upon which we all depend.

Paul As An MSC

Jim Littleton MSC

I first knew Paul Stenhouse in 1955 when, not much older than he, I taught him Ancient History at the Sacred Heart Apostolic School at Douglas Park. He became a Missionary of the Sacred Heart when he took his first vows in a Profession Ceremony on February 26, 1957. He was ordained as an MSC priest on July 7, 1963

Over most of his life Paul and I have been close friends. We have travelled together by car through much of Australia and we have also travelled overseas together. As Missionaries of the Sacred Heart we shared a common aspiration to make the Heart of Jesus better known throughout the world. Paul did this in many admirable and remarkable ways.

As editor for about 50 years Paul brought the message of God's love to numerous people. In the early years there was a catechetical supplement which applied the teachings of the Second Vatican Council to current catechetics to assist Religious Education teachers in many schools, both Catholic and otherwise. In later years the Annals contributed to explaining and maintaining Catholic culture.

I have always admired the way in which Paul could produce ten issues of the *Annals* each year while being involved in so many other ministries. When he was in good health there was rarely an evening on which he was not visiting someone in need of assistance, particularly international students who did not know how to cope with demands of departmental authorities. This sometimes led to marriages and baptisms and was MSC ministry at a practical level.

I also admired Paul's erudition, evident in his three-volume doctoral thesis on a piece of Samaritan literature. This was evident too in his writings on Middle Eastern history and politics where he was much better informed than most journalists throughout the country. It was evident again in the many articles that he contributed to the *Annals* on religious, ecclesiastical and political issues. It was as an MSC that he wrote these articles and he examined them in the light of the MSC charism.

Missionaries of the Sacred Heart have always been involved in a variety of personal ministries One that was unique to Paul, because of his love for the Church was his involvement with Aid to the Church in Need. For several years he was chairman of the Australian branch of this worldwide organisation and a member of the International Council.

At its peak in the post-Vatican II era the *Annals* had a wider circulation than any other journal in Australia. In later years it had financial problems, but Paul always had trust that God would work things out and it did. He had many benefactors who appreciated his ministry. Paul's commitment to the *Annals* was evident in his last weeks on earth when he was determined to bring out its last issue before he died some days later.

Paul lived at Kensington Monastery for almost all of his priestly life. It was home to him. He extolled its merits and made visitors welcome. He was faithful to daily Mass and in his homilies could always say something that was different and interesting. It was always evident that God was central to his life and that God's love encompassed all things. The hundreds of people who attended his Funeral Mass was testimony to the way in which Paul had touched their lives and to the high esteem in which he was held.

Jim Littleton MSC

Paul: A Personal Memoir

Peter Malone MSC

Not sure about first impressions! A new group of postulants, January 1957, we stood on the back of the truck from Douglas Park station, over the ford of the Nepean River, up the hill and along the drive towards the main building of St Mary's Towers. The novice master, Father Frank Butler, stood in formal line with the novices as we passed along, shaking hands with each, being welcomed. Paul was part of that group of novices.

Formation Years

He was about to complete the novitiate, professing his first vows on February 26th. He had spent some time in the apostolic school so was familiar with the novitiate building, the wooden 'Ark', on the other side of the hedge from the school. The novitiate began with an eight-day retreat, daily strict regime, conferences on the Constitutions, Latin classes, manual work in the garden, the vegetable gardens, the chook houses ... There was also the formal 'Chapter of Faults', every Friday morning, speaking out loud some external faults. Father Butler's spirituality was one of bending our wills by private and public humiliations. Not that there weren't some cheery moments! But, no visitors. No radio. No newspapers. Writing home regularly and some letters in return.

In the August of his novitiate year, Paul and his fellow-novices made a 30-day retreat, the 'Long Retreat' following the pattern of the Spiritual Exercises of St Ignatius Loyola. Quite some intense spiritual formation, cut off from the world, prayer, silence, and experience of inner and exterior earnestness.

My next meeting with Paul was after profession, travelling to the Sacred Heart Monastery at Croydon, Victoria. After the novitiate, there were many, many breaths of fresh air, sometimes literal as we worked outside, went for a bike rides or walks twice a week (the jargon was 'stunts'), played football and basketball. In fact, I worked with Paul not outside but in the basement, in the bookbinding room. Probably the way that I got to know him first and more closely.

In 1960, because the scholastic at Croydon was so crowded with students (most of us not having our own room for our first two years but sleeping in dormitory-like conditions in balconies and parlours, doing our studies down in the classrooms) that a new philosophy house was opened in Canberra. But, while the routines of the scholasticate can look formal and strict in retrospect, there was a certain feeling of liberation (although, wearing shorts was forbidden and there was a campaign 'Shorts for Shoreham!', our holiday house).

Also in retrospect, study standard was very high and Paul excelled in studies. In the first three years, the focus was on philosophy, ethics, Church history and Old Testament Studies (Paul always acknowledged John Savage's skills in communicating philosophy, Dennis Murphy with Scripture). After three years, there was theology, especially with Jim Cuskelly and his spirituality expertise, and, as Director of Students, his excellent 20-minute conferences twice a week.

Dennis Murphy continued with the New Testament. There was Moral Theology, Canon Law, Homiletics. We read widely. We produced our own magazines, *Stella Matutina* and *Theologian*. There were four full-length plays produced every year. There were a scratch concerts, Eistedfodds in the mid winter holidays as well as reading novels (no such thing as television). Paul was musical, lots of choir rehearsals and ceremonies, plain chant, polyphony—and sometimes performing with our other singers Gilbert and Sullivan.

The great break was six weeks' holiday, January–February, at The Cliffs, at Shoreham on Westernport Bay. I do remember in 1959, Paul, Leo Hill and myself, finishing cleaning up at 11.00 am and then riding back to Croydon, a long route through Beaconsfield and Emerald, 75 miles.

Speaking of plays, Paul was the Director for 1962. We didn't have such big numbers, so we had several opportunities for performances, Peter Ustinov's *Romanoff and Juliet* and Robert Bolt's *A Man for All Seasons*. They were very effective productions and performances as well as staging and costumes and I had an opportunity to be Henry VIII with Ted Collins (later Bishop of Darwin) as St Thomas More.

I want to say something about Mrs Stenhouse. She was something of a large presence, in every sense. When I was sent to Rome in 1962, Paul suggested that Dad and I visit his mother at Camden. This was beginning of a long friendship between Mrs Stenhouse and my family, especially my grandmother and aunt, Sheila. Looking at letters from these times, I see many references to Mrs Stenhouse and I received many from her, usually with Mass offerings, a quotation from some Catholic author, like Lacordaire, and her signing off with affection. It was easy to see where Paul inherited his love of literature, language, history. When my grandmother was ill, Paul celebrated Mass at our home. I see from a letter that he wrote as early as 1964 that he used to drop in to see my grandmother and Sheila—'I feel very much at home when I visit'. When my grandmother died, he went into action immediately, with the organisation of the Requiem Mass and funeral.

Tony Arthur was very kind when his mother died and Mrs Stenhouse was able to go to Earlwood to live in Mrs Arthur's house. Her final years were spent at the Little Sisters of the Poor at Drummoyne. Just a word about Paul's brother, Richard, whose family Paul regularly visited on those nocturnal trips around Sydney. We were amused when Richard became engaged to Gloria and the newspapers highlighted the engagement, Stenhouse-Woodhouse.

Ministry, and Annals

Returning from Rome in 1966, my connections with Paul were renewed, especially with *Annals,* his asking me to write a series of articles on the Second Vatican Council. 'Can you write something on Ecumenism in Rome'. This was the time when he began his long editorship of the magazine, reshaped it in many ways, began a decade of Catechetical Supplements. He had been influenced very much by the Josephite religious education expert, Sister Peter at North Sydney. Paul had had very little contact with nuns and religious brothers in his early years but discovered many of them (many oppressed by parish priests as he would often say) and enlisted their considerable help in preparing the Supplements. There were also a number of MSC, especially Frank Fletcher who had previously published articles on counselling in *Annals*. If one were to look back at some of the Supplements and accompanying articles in those years, they would find quite a number of quotations from teenagers, both boys and girls, insightful, often expressions of hopes and desires. Many of them were, in fact, written by Kevin Bowden who was teaching at Daramalan College and then at Holy Cross Woollahra. Paul supported Kevin strongly. I don't think many people knew of this at the time.

Paul asked me to write a lot of the Teachers' Guides for the Supplements and I have many memories of Mass supply in Lilydale Parish, between Masses, parked outside the Wandin church, writing these Guides in longhand. We were in our 30s and this kind of enterprise was exhilarating. However, one year, it was not easy, teaching Scripture and theology at the Monastery in Canberra and some part-time teaching at Daramalan, when Paul contracted the mumps and entrusted me to see through the publication of the August 1970 issue. Yes, we were young and enthusiastic.

I'd better say something about the movie reviews. In 1967, Paul featured several articles on religious films of those years including *A Man for Seasons, The Gospel According to Matthew*. In discussing films with him, I offered to write some film reviews, the first being *To Sir with Love*. However, he published an introductory review, of the musical, *Camelot*. It was headed 'The Glory that was *Camelot* (almost)'. His rather negative take on *Camelot* almost killed off the reviews before they started. Warner Brothers publicity not happy. However, I was happy to do the reviews from 1968–1998. The only time Paul ever changed a review was to modify *The Last Temptation of Christ* and some historical detail for *Queen Margot*. Otherwise they all were published without change.

I soon discovered Paul's taste in films, very action-oriented, when we went to see Laurence Olivier in Chekhov's *Three Sisters*, which ran for 2½ hours. And he fidgeted, rattling his keys almost all the way through. Yes, action-oriented from then on. On a visit to Bill Collins' home, we enjoyed a screening of Quentin Durward in his home theatre—and Channel 7 copy with blank frames in those days for the commercials and, at each break, Bill enthusing about what was to come, We attended a number of previews. I remember going with him to *Rosemary's Baby*, wearing clericals, and the columnist for the back page of *The Australian* the next morning stating that two priests were seen to leave the preview—without comment. Nobody asked us.

Generally, it was only after the event, that Paul published editorials explaining some of the moral repercussions of the reviews, and inviting me to write articles on *Morals and Movies*, only for me to find out afterwards that there had been complaints, some Episcopal, and that he had answered them on my behalf.

The other aspect of his work in the *Annals* Office was his establishing of Chevalier Press. He was very good to me in publishing the first Chevalier Press book, *The Film*, released in 1971, then two volumes of *200 Movies and Discussions*. It was the beginning of many decades of publications, background to the Catechetical Supplements, in booklets of commentary on literature and history for secondary schools, *Literary Perspectives*, *Historical Perspectives*. Chevalier Press would publish all of Michael Fallon's commentaries on Scripture as well as a number of booklets, *Why Do Catholics'* and a series of ten which might be labelled as 'popular apologetics', *Understanding Catholicism* by Paul himself.

In 1967, Denis Murphy had established the theological review, *Compass*. It was taken on by Spectrum Publications, rather than by the Province. When Dennis asked me to be editor in 1972, it seemed a good idea to have discussions with John Ostermeir, owner of Spectrum, for *Compass* to become part of Chevalier Press. This happened in 1973 with Paul becoming Executive Editor and contributing articles over the decades. He immediately fostered interfaith dialogue with a series of articles on Biblical Archeology by his friend, Professor Alan Crown of Sydney University. (1972–98, I was editor, followed by Barry Brundell, 1999–2016, when the decision was made to close publication after a good run of 50 years—and the ever-increasing prevalence of online theology.)

I should add that Paul kept an eye on Chevalier Press from Rome and from the Balkans during the years he was away, wanting to hear news of how Geoff Baumgardner was managing the *Annals*, the Catechetical Supplements, the Chevalier Bookshop, now established in the Kensington monastery building. During those years I was ultimately responsible for Chevalier Press—and they were difficult years, after a successful series of Supplements on Scripture, there was a downfall with Moral Theology, complaints from Monsignor Kevin Toomey from Melbourne, an emergency meeting with Dennis Murphy in 1980, the decision to close the Supplements, especially had as we had moved on to the difficult areas of sexuality (and, the March 1980 issue, with its supplement on issues of Masturbation, must have been one of the few editions to be sent out early, before Dennis decided to pulp the issue!). And Paul returned in 1981, a meeting with Dennis, Geoff and myself, and the decision for Paul to resume the editorship.

Later Ministry

During the 1980s, Paul often spent summer holiday days with me at the Hour Lady of the Missions house in Mount Eliza. One reason for remembering this is an occasion where we were talking about his work with *Annals* and Chevalier Press. At the National Pastoral Institute, we had spent some time with the Belbin Inventory and a questionnaire for us to investigate priorities in how people could work together. Paul filled in the form—but the results were skewiff, made no sense at all, and we realised that he was a one-man band, which could be disconcerting. Which may be an indication as to why he found it very difficult at times living in community, understanding some regulations, opposing what he thought was over-regulation.

It was also at this time that we began an enthusiasm for the Myers Briggs Type Indicator (MBTI). He was very quick on the uptake and enthusiastically identified with extraversion. One of the characteristics of extraversion is that the extrovert draws energy and zest from the outer world, events, contact with people, more than from the inner world—and most of us would agree that Paul and his range of contact with people was an extrovert off the page!

Paul had an enormous and fruitful ministry with the Chinese and other Asian families in Sydney. I would like to take some credit for this—a very, very indirect influence. In 1979, Paul and I travelled from Rome back to Australia, some adventures in Athens which was full of Americans, allegedly working for the Bell Phone Company in Iran, but, it turned out that this was the period of the Iranian revolution and one presumes that the Bell Company was a cover for intelligence agents.

We experienced a difficulty in Athens, our connecting plane to Istanbul snowed in in Brussels and Paul deciding we should go by bus instead. We travelled by night. In the morning at the Greek/Turkish border, quite isolated, the bus was stopped, only eight of us midwinter, but those with Greek passports travelling to Turkey had their suitcases opened and everything emptied onto the highway. The guards then played baseball for several hours as we waited, then we had to change buses, no Greek buses into Turkey, no Turkish buses into Greece, and eventually arrived in Istanbul, an old hotel with cockroaches in the shower. We searched, unsuccessfully, for the site of the Council of Nicaea—but were amazed to see hundreds of workers as we waited for a ferry all wrapped watching the small television screen on the upper wall: the Benny Hill program!

We flew from Istanbul to Tel Aviv, Turkish security, then stricter El Al security, arriving at the eve of sabbath, moving into the hostel of the Sisters of, and, for me, a wonderful 10 days of being guided by Paul through Israel, absorbing the spirit in the spirituality of Jesus walking the earth.

Perhaps I have been carried away a bit, but here is the part about Asia. We had to fly back to Rome because Iranian airspace was not available. Our destination was Bombay, before Mumbai, and staying with a community of Christian Brothers, five Indian, one Irish, six Irish accents! We went by train to Poona, wanting to buy economy class but advised by the ticket seller to go first class. Outside the station we could see what 2 in 10,000 meant as we mingled with the locals. This was Paul's first introduction to Asia, and it had a profound consequent effect. It meant almost 40 years of ministering to Asians in Sydney and beyond, frequent visits to various countries in Asia, a service to the students at the University of New South Wales, the Asian Catholic community in Randwick and many, many others. A key part of his ministry from 1979 to his death.

I don't know whether this story is on record that is. He received a phone call from Mother Teresa at the General House in 1978. She wanted him to give a retreat to the novices. He didn't want to and tried to gain some time by saying he would have to ask his superior. Paul said she was a bit taken aback and told him that Alitalia that day was flying donkeys to the Sudan for her. When she rang again, he said the superior told him no. She then asked him to give some conferences instead to the novices. Relieved, he agreed. She told him the first one was to be the next day!

During the 1980s and 1990s, I saw Paul only on visits to Sydney, sitting in his room, listening to tryouts of articles, finding an action film to review at the Showground Cinemas or East Gardens, and always the offer of the lift to the airport. Melbourne was not one of his favourite cities to visit, so we didn't see him there.

From 1999–2010, I was based at Nazareth house in Hammersmith, London. We found Paul's autograph in the visitors' book, from 1977. That reminded him that when members of the Nazareth Sisters' General Council, whose mother house was in Hammersmith, visited Rome, he used to drive them from the airport to their destination. In those years, he was very much involved in Aid to the Church in Need, going to several meetings a year to their central offices in Germany. Which meant that he stayed with me two or three times a year for all those years. And we had a certain ritual, at least one meal out, at McDonald's, and checking out where there was an action film that we could go to. He had a huge repertoire of stories about Aid to the Church in Need meetings, visiting various countries which had received grants, visiting different office bearers in England. On one visit, we did branch out, a train trip to visit Canterbury and back.

It was more than a shock to see him at St Vincent's Hospital in 2012 with the diagnosis of cancer, with the surgery. Which means that he had seven years living with cancer and its consequences, often in pain, the inconvenience of the catheter, finding himself sick one time when we were later in Hammersmith, unable to get a plane seat to return to Australia for a week. During his last years, there was a repetition of my visits to Sydney, sitting in his room, his trying out his articles, especially his series on Islam, a film, the lift back to the airport.

I do regret that I did not see him for a year before he died. He had, in fact, visited Melbourne for the Requiem mass for our confrere Peter Wood, somebody he admired. (And, I was able to return the courtesy by getting him to the airport after the mass.) So my communication with him during 2019 was by phone. At one stage, he wanted to get the email address of the superior of the Nazareth Sisters at Hammersmith, a final visit to the UK—stating that he might as well be sick in London as at Kensington. But the last phone call, in the last month, was asking me to cancel his visit. I was surprised at the change of tone of his voice, faltering, the lack of energy.

His vigil at Kensington monastery was impressive, the range of people who spoke, honouring him, remembering him, his personality, his extraordinary outreach, his kindness which was ever-obliging, and his role as a priest. The church of Our Lady of the Rosary, Kensington Parish, was full, MSC, diocesan and religious clergy, Anthony Fisher, Archbishop of Sydney, his brother, Richard and the family, and his many, many friends.

I was asked to say a few words at Douglas Park before his burial—and my theme has become the title of this book, Paul Stenhouse , a distinctive and distinguished Missionary of the Sacred Heart.

MEMORIES AND CONNECTIONS

Tricia Kavanagh

I write not of the Priest known to all as an intellectual, a lecturer in Samaritan Studies, a writer, a journalist, a man with the gift of tongues but rather of Father Paul—a mentor, at times a tormentor, a family member, the family priest and my dear friend.

When did this friendship begin? I cannot remember the date, nor the year but it was somewhere around 1965. I knew him then as a relative—Dad has a cousin relationship with his mother, Mai Stenhouse—a marvelous, eccentric woman. Paul lived in the Monastery of the Missionaries of the Sacred Heart (the 'MSCs'), on the Hill at Kensington, and came down the hill to our home for Sunday lunch. Baked chicken and Mum's apple pie served at the big table always set to welcome country relatives, their lost kids in the city (maybe in those early days Paul was one) and other visitors—the latter often friends from Dad's world—pubs and the racing! Regularly Paul just rang the doorbell, instinctively right on time and joined us for lunch or, at other times, just rang the doorbell and had a cup of tea with Mum whom he really loved.

After a few years teaching, then travel overseas and my return to these shores we met up again. I was a little lost and not sure if I wanted to go back to teaching—the wild, wide world had captured my imagination and it was hard to settle. Paul was the editor of the *Annals* and completing his thesis for his BA (Hons) under (Emeritus) Professor Alan Crown, head of SemItic Studies at Sydney University. Later, of Alan, Paul said 'he was an exceptional person. There was in fact nothing average about him at all.' The same could be said of Paul, as he himself was soon to discover.

The *Annals* was thriving in the early 70s under his editorial guidance but Paul was still a one-man band. He nominated his topics, chose his contributors, set out the content, did the page layout then, in my day, took the drive up the road parallel to the railway line to Lidcombe to the printer. He even set the print font for every article and heading. After proof reading the first copy, back up to Lidcombe then corrections and the run. He called upon the people whose minds interested him. He picked his topics (read magazine content) and searched for willing souls who would make a contribution to any debate he excited. His focus was, in these times, on education and the curious mind. Such a broad all—encompassing ambit ensured no topic was out of bounds for the *Annals*!!

But after I joined him—as a dogsbody to allow him the occasional free moment to complete his Thesis we had such fun. I arrived up the Monastery in a road registered canary yellow, beach buggy. Just before he died, he spoke of it and our mutual regret neither of us had a photo (I am sure if we had one it would have been discretely placed in the last edition!). Our routine was: I would drive up to the Monastery, walk along the grand corridor of exquisite, tessellated tiles, head cast down to avoid eye contact with the elderly priests who saw me as an invader of their treasured monastic life, climb up that imposing staircase whose treads were slippery from wear, tiptoe along the rough and creaking wooden floorboards on the second floor and into a tiny room in the attic right hand corner. In the room there was a desk for me against the hallway wall measuring about 3 foot, a chair and when the chair was out from the desk his table rested against the back of my chair. On his table was his Thesis, which involved the translation of an Arabic Samaritan document from the early ages. Later when translating another Middle Ages Samaritan text for his PhD he declared there could perhaps be a little bias in the reporting of early events in our Christian literature! Each day there would be a list on my desk of the oddest of tasks (I loved reading his instructions as they always differed and gave promise of an interesting day) as Paul, up early and having already said Mass and put in a couple of hours work, was ready for his escape and a swim. He would take off in that buggy with great joy. He had already begun his ministry in support for Chinese students at the University of NSW and would often drag one or two into the buggy for a swim.

Years later I was up visiting him and he excitedly showed me his new office. A grand room on the first floor: a large credenza and sitting in the middle of it a huge computer screen and on the hutch a TV always turned on and playing the Al Jazeera TV Channel which he listened to in Arabic ' you always need to know what is really going on' he would say! Travelling along and up each side of the office were bookshelves from floor to ceiling and now he had his library of precious books around him. The room had wonderful light and the most magnificent and grand set of library steps with a platform. He could stand up there searching or reading for hours. Paul had no sense of possession, nor of ownership, nor did he seek material apparel (always looking slightly ragged) but he literally loved his library of research books and those library steps. A most thoughtful patron and skilled craftsman had made them for him!

I need to mention the gratitude and love that Paul felt for the MSCs. It was not only for his education in faith and knowledge but at a personal level. During a time when his mother was growing old and frail and needed care but was also wildly independent (just like Paul) the Order rescued him. Her need for care struck Paul and he spent agonizing hours wondering how he could help her. She lived out her life in a home inherited by an MSC priest. It passed to the Order only after her death.

In those early days Paul was discovering the ambit of his intellect and, with a faith that never faulted, he was on his search for knowledge. His faith was grounded from his mother, as was his intellect. He saw an advertisement as a young 16-year-old printer 'Get yourself an Education—join the MSCs'. Through his early studies under the guidance of MSC scholars that faith became his bedrock which enabled him, as the world slowly opened up before him, to enjoy it but with a deep discernment. Truth was his guide and metre. But the practice of his faith through his priestly work was always based on an acute social awareness. His family struggled, as he has written. He was, in those days, as he was throughout his pastoral life, very socially conscious and caring. Many of the students to whom he ministered graduated, stayed in Australia and he became priest to their families and then their children's families. They were there with him throughout his long illness. I must mention his courage in ill health. His work ethic never failed him. The physical discomfort was enormous, the treatments so painful: but he just soldiered on. The nursing sister caring for him in his last days said simply 'he has the heart of a horse—it just will not give up.' Paul would have liked that !

Some of his published obituaries were from the intellectual right and fulsome in their praise. But they rather stole the Paul we knew. Certainly, he was proudly conservative in support of the Church he loved and reared up to defend it if there was any negative inference cast upon it. He did not hesitate to meet head on any direct attack with very lucid and persuasive argument. He was a true intellectual warrior for the Church. But I also recall his friendships with persons so diverse: with Rupert Lockwood of the Petrov Royal Commission fame. Rupert, a journalist, was the alleged author of Document J and the cross examination of him as to his knowledge of the workings of the Communist Party in Australia was rigorous: the man of whom (then) Barwick QC, Counsel Assisting, praised as 'the only witness I could not break.' We had some wonderful and stimulating meals and arguments with Rupert and his good friend, the Plumber and their raggedy friends up at Spencer in Rupert's house on the Macdonald River above the Hawkesbury. Paul was fascinated by persons who had the quality of Leadership. He was drawn to Leaders in all walks of life including those in politics, academia and the entertainment industry: Fr Peter Malone MSC and I joined him as he tried to set up an interview with Topol the star of *Fiddler on the Roof*. At the pending press conference Paul disappeared and when Topol walked onto the stage Paul was with him, both chatting away in Hebrew. Paul had his interview! I often wondered why we had such press access and asked a publicity girl at the theatre who replied, 'your magazine is lifeblood to us— those theatre reviews, if supportive, bring bus-loads of school children to our productions'. Paul discovered Bill Collins, Mr Movies, and I recall many visits to his home, where he then lived with his Mum who was always pouring us cups of tea as Bill played one of his extraordinary collection of old, classic movies from a home projector onto the lounge room wall.

The years drew Paul's focus onto serious world events and I think, in those later years, as many burdens weighed upon him, those early memories became a distraction for him. He enjoyed the retelling during his last days. The work for the MSCs was always his priority and I sing the praises of the MSC Order. There was never any corralling of, or judgement cast upon, Paul for his individuality—the leadership of the MSC's supported him and his international ministry flourished. He gave back to them: the Church and his Order, with his love and service. I know the Order's monetary support for the *Annals* weighed upon him. He was resigned at the end to its closure but was determined to put it to bed in his own timing. He settled the last edition along with his own death in the same week. But in its content the *Annals* monthly magazine was extraordinary: its topics were wide ranging. Women were given a voice as to the challenges they faced in their role as Catholic mothers; women's active role within the church hierarchy was supported; the Arts were always given a voice; modern political issues were addressed through thoughtful articles written by experts (some were his own). His disdain for the western, military intervention in the Middle East is there in his writings and of the Syria intervention he said 'careful what you wish for!' He extended The *Annals* reach into other publications and Chevalier Press was born. The booklet in which he recently published a collation of his series of articles on Middle Eastern politics and the rise and challenge of Islam (with its internal struggles) is a readable but rigorous revelation of past events and predicts future consequences. Scholars now rely upon it. How the right could see him only as their champion made me wonder did they read! One journalist with puzzlement mentioned his friendship with a serious, left wing Labor intellectual from WA, Senator John Wheeldon. They told me they would be attending a conference once and without any guidance I found them sitting up the front at a Fallangist conference in the outskirts of Paris enjoying the loud cacophony of Arabic argument. But Paul's existence there was related to the very serious work he did carrying vital medications from Cyprus by ferry to the Lebanon shores during the Civil Wars. We worried for his safety. As we did when as the Board member of Aid to The Church in Need, he travelled through China and assessed the state of the underground Christian movement. The Church was recommended to settle the internal Catholic Bishops fuddle and Paul carried to the reconstituted Bishops the papal investiture and imprimaturs to validate their authority. When the Syrian conflict erupted he returned home frustrated he couldn't get into Aleppo! Paul may have always looked like Mr Average but his gift of tongues and his deep-seated modesty, not to mention his casual presence, ensured he never looked a threat in conflict zones and, in those, he did much of his work. But it also broke his caring heart. In his last years there was a lot of cursing—'Mother Machree'—and the frown grew deeper as his worldly experiences took their heavy toll.

He wanted more from this world and his later writings carry warnings. Yet, who didn't enjoy the benefit of his knowledge and generosity with that one thing he treasured most: 'time'. Did he not always have a moment of time—perhaps just to take you quickly to visit the Archbasilica of St John Lateran, the Cathedral Church of the Diocese of Rome, in the city of Rome, which serves as the seat of the Pontiff. Just so you could touch its bronze Roman Senate doors?!

On a lighter note our family, as did others, remember our wonderful family priest. I went to Paul when I was to be married, registering a small problem as I felt the political disapproval of our local Parish Priest to my marriage to the local State Member of Parliament. Paul disappeared for a time and on return announced, to my astonishment, we had permission to marry in the Monastery! We were the first wedding in that Chapel and what a blessing—I still recall walking down the aisle at dusk, the setting sun striking the stained-glass windows above the altar—the Chapel ablaze with coloured sunbeams. The Chapel became the site of many family ceremonies thereafter: the christening of our sons, their marriages, the christening of their children and that of our niece, her children and her grandchild. Paul prayed over some very sad funerals as we lost our parents, a brother and a sister. I recall his words at our Mum's funeral where he was the principal celebrant but spoke as a family member. He caught my mother's spirit in the words 'hands up any here present who have not had the honour of being pulled into line by Nora!' Less than a month before he died, Paul christened our youngest grandchild. He was frail and he had to pause the ceremony: yet with that falter, a huge surge of love poured over Paul in that Chapel—you could feel it. We sat together afterwards he and I and dear Brother Boland in the sacristy. Paul could barely talk. I found him the next day. 'Just a hiccup', he said. He has shared all our family's joys and sorrows for over 55 years.

I think now in wonder of the year or so I worked with Paul. What lives we have enjoyed. I remember old Father Rumble MSC, a hero in the days of the Labor Party split who argued with Archbishop Mannix, using his media strength as the first media savvy priest on radio. When I wondered out loud to Paul what did he think Doc Rumble was burning off in the incinerator (placed with the best view to the south at the corner of the Monastery where the car park is now), Paul took off, his Thesis hitting the ground. I still wonder how much of the historical collection of Doc Rumble's words and work lies singed or blackened in the MSC's archives.

Paul visited, as usual, fairly recently and was carrying his Academic gown and mortar. We had our morning coffee, croissant, then his toast and marmalade. A chat about the state of the world; a quick recommendation, to be carried as advice for the latest leader of the Labor Party; analysis of the state of the country; enquiry as to the fate of all the children in the family and then the quick take off. He was always the Will o' the Wisp, sometimes bringing someone we should meet: never staying long, always staying in touch. My favourite possession—he left me his academic robes on his last visit that morning. Paul had a brother he loved but the brother used to say to me 'Where did he come from? How could we be so different?' Paul loved Richard but they were very different. However, he grew very close to his nephew and his daughters. As those girls go to Uni and begin their careers, they shall inherit these robes. May they meet his standards of excellence. So he was proud of me? The frown if my language was sharp, the questioning of my judgement or opinion with that frown, the red pen to anything I wrote for him. A lifetime of mentoring.

Rest in peace, my dear friend, Father Paul.

A Memory

Anthony Brereton

Around 2008 I was a primary school teacher at St Finbar's Sans Souci. In the lead up to the September Feast Day of Saint Finbar I visited Fr Paul in his Monastery office and explained that little information was available about Saint Finbar (born AD 550). Father Paul listened patiently, then climbed his library ladder and pulled down a bound volume from a set of about two dozen. He explained that this was an Encyclopedia set written by Jesuits near Belgium in the 1870s. He then opened the book to the entry for Saint Finbar.

Father Paul then took a knife and began cutting the folded page. I asked what he was doing. Paul explained that the text was made by hand and the paper had been folded and bound into a book and over the last century no-one had opened this particular page, so the page was still folded from printing. Paul smiled and assured me there is no damage in cutting the pages and that books are made to be read.

Father Paul then read the Latin text and translated the story of Saint Finbar to me in English. There was an interesting aside conversation about problems of Gaelic translations into Latin and Paul even went so far as to apologise for not knowing the translation of two Gaelic words.

I often visited Father Paul for a chat, and he was always kind, helpful and interested in talking about learning, pedagogy and faith. But this was the only time that he cut the pages of a century old text, translating over three languages just to help a 30-year-old primary school teacher find out some facts about a Saint who lived 1500 years ago.

Vale, Father Paul

Recollections

John S. Madden

When I was in Sixth Form in 1968 at Saint Joseph's College, Hunters Hill, just after breakfast one morning a few days before Easter, I walked past and exchanged greetings with a young visiting priest whom I later learned was Father Paul Stenhouse. That exchange lasted no more than three seconds and little did I anticipate that within a few years Paul would become my closest friend.

In January 1969 I joined the Missionaries of the Sacred Heart to begin religious formation and studies for the priesthood. In early January 1972 I went to Sacred Heart Monastery, Kensington, to do odd jobs over the weeks before the new study year began. I went there again in the early weeks of 1973 and 1974. Most of my time at Kensington was spent helping Paul in one way or another in the Annals Office which in those days also served as his bedroom. I ran errands, checked galley proofs, tracked down photographs, delivered packages late at night to the courier in Mascot just in time to catch the last truck so that material would arrive at the printer interstate the following morning. One year Paul had me paint his bedroom from top to bottom; the Superior of the house, Father Mortimer Kerrins, was a little surprised by his choice of colour, lilac.

On most nights there would be a knock on my door and Paul would say, 'C'mon, Giovanni. Let's go and visit some friends of mine.' We would speed around Sydney and suburbs with Paul slamming on the brakes at red traffic lights; it was not in his repertoire to ease the brakes on as we approached. He knew all the back roads and short cuts. We would visit three or four families in a night. No matter how late we called we were always made welcome. Paul's friends were people in all of life's situations from struggling, to making ends meet, to well-to-do, from the lowly to the highly-placed. I once asked Paul how he came to know and be good friends with so many and such different types of people; he replied, 'Believe me, Giovanni, many people who are friends to me would not be were I not a Catholic priest'. He taught me much in those wild rides. To me he seemed to me to know everything about everything, but when I suggested that, he replied that he just talked a lot about the little he did know.

Late one night we stopped off at a cafe in North Sydney. The doors were open, the lights were on, there were no customers, the proprietor was busy behind the counter. Paul stepped up and ordered a couple of cups of tea. 'Sorry, mate, tea's off!' came the reply. 'But, but, can't you boil some water or something?!' expostulated Paul, 'Who's ever heard of tea being off!'. The tea, which Paul preferred very weak but with plenty of leaves, was served with no further objection.

From time to time we would go to dinner at the late Bill Collins' home in Jannali after which Bill would take us down to his backyard movie theatre and say, 'Well, what would you like to see?' Bill's studio was packed to the rafters with 16mm reels of film and LPs of movie soundtracks, not to mention movie posters, books and a great variety of other movie memorabilia.

On return to Kensington I would go straight to bed but

Paul would return to his desk for more work. He would go to bed around 1:00 or 2:00 am and would be up only 4 or 5 hours later when he would celebrate a private Mass and then be back at his desk to begin another day's work. That work habit went on for many years; I do not know how he survived and produced so much of quality after so little sleep. Paul's mother was also something of a night owl and they would often speak on the telephone sometime between midnight and 1:00 in the morning.

I left the MSCs midway through 1974, nevertheless the friendship between Paul and me continued unbroken until his death.

When he was in Rome for some years as secretary to the Superior-General, Father Jim Cuskelly, Paul spent many hours showing my parents, to whom he was also a good friend, all sorts of things both on and off the tourist track when they visited there in 1977. Frantically busy as he always was, Paul's generosity to others was unstinting.

Just one of so many little acts of kindness that I witnessed over the years and recall was when, in bucketing rain in George Street a few years before his death, he noticed an elderly lady without an umbrella vainly trying to hail a taxi cab. Paul ushered her to shelter in a shop doorway, stepped out into the deluge, successfully hailed a cab and helped the lady into it. Would I have been so chivalrous had Paul not been there?

If I wanted a book that I could not track down in Australia he would, during a fleeting visit to London, go out of his way to Foyle's on Charing Cross Road to buy it for me.

I had only to pick up the telephone for him cheerfully to

answer a query on a point of grammar, pronunciation (he was the only person I have ever known to utter the word 'enclitic') or punctuation, for example whether a full stop should be placed before or after the inverted comma at the end of a sentence. And Paul would call me to ask my opinion about something or other; that could sometimes be a frustrating exercise. He called me about a year before he died wanting to know what I thought a certain part of a hand-written text, that he had before him and which he found indecipherable, could possibly say. 'It looks like ... ' he repeated, to which I replied, 'Paulo, depending on whether or not I know something about its subject matter, it might look like something entirely different to me.' But no, he did not have time to scan and email the text to me. We got nowhere.

There was never an occasion that I was departing for or returning from overseas that Paul was not at Sydney Airport to see me off or to welcome me home.

Paul never rejected anyone's call for help. He was often called upon to give character references for people convicted of criminal offences, further evidence of the variety of Paul's friendships. He was kindly known amongst some members of the Sydney Bar as 'rent-a-priest'. On one occasion an investigating detective got wind of the fact that Paul was to be called as a character witness for the convicted. He rang Paul to remonstrate with him, saying 'You're on his side!' Pauls response was typical, 'For God's sake, I'm a priest! If someone asks for my help, I can't turn my back on him.'

Paul's love of languages is well known, his own native tongue and others, especially Latin, Italian, French, Hebrew, Arabic, Aramaic. Quite often over the years, either face to face or over the telephone, he would read out a passage in say Hebrew, of which I know nothing, and say, 'Isn't that beautiful!' He was referring not only to the idea expressed but to the very sound of it. Because of my indolence his many attempts over many years to encourage me to resume the study of Latin fell on deaf ears.

In 2013 Paul and I began to meet for lunch about every three weeks in Berrima, he driving from Sydney and I from Canberra. Now and again, on impulse, I would call him and suggest we meet on a weekday as well. In 2014 we discovered *Josh's Cafe* which immediately became our favourite haunt and where we went exclusively from then on. Those meetings with Paul in Berrima were the highlight of my life. Very often one or both of us would have an unusual book to show the other. We talked of, laughed about and lamented many things. We always made the Sign of the Cross and said Grace before Meals in Latin; we did not mind who noticed, although I admit that I always felt slightly sheepish.

Nothing was ever too much trouble for Paul. On one occasion, about a year before he died, I was driving to Berrima to meet him for lunch in a Subaru Outback purchased new, when the engine 'blew up' about half way between Goulburn and Berrima. I rang Paul on his mobile phone to tell him that our meeting was off and that he should turn back to Kensington, which he did. He asked me to let him know the diagnosis when the NRMA arrived. The car was not driveable and so it and me were taken back to Goulburn by tow truck. I rang Paul, who had then been back at Kensington for about three hours, to explain the situation and tell him that I would catch a bus or a train back to Canberra the following day. He would not hear of it and insisted on driving immediately to Goulburn to drive me back to Canberra.

Paul and Cardinal George Pell were very good friends. They would occasionally go for dinner at *Alfredo's Bulletin Place* restaurant in the city. Paul had a grace and favour car park at St. Mary's Cathedral so he would drive to the Cathedral and from there he and the Cardinal would walk down Macquarie Street to 16 Bulletin Place. When they arrived, the proprietor, Alfredo, would always seat them at the rear of the restaurant, at a table situated on a slightly raised platform against a wall which was draped from ceiling to floor with a big red curtain. From there Paul and the Cardinal had a fine view down the length of the restaurant. And of course, the other patrons had a fine view of them! Cardinal Pell was appointed Prefect of the Secretariat for the Economy of the Holy See in February of 2014. During his absence in Rome, Paul and I went for dinner at Alfredo's on one occasion, parking the car at St Mary's and following the same route down to the restaurant. Upon our arrival Alfredo seated us at the table usually reserved for Paul and the Cardinal. We had a wonderful evening but, when we were departing Alfredo refused to let me pay the bill saying that our evening was on him in honour of Cardinal Pell.

Paul was, of course, devoted to the *Annals*; it was his primary ministry. Paul's generosity meant that many people were the recipients of free subscriptions. Not surprisingly, towards the end of the *Annals'* life, and of Paul's, it was running out of money. I tried to urge him that the price of an annual subscription was ridiculously low and that he should increase it; after all the price of a subscription approximated to that of a packet of cigarettes, but he would not be persuaded saying that it was not a problem of price but of circulation.

After God, the Catholic Church was Paul's greatest love. He wrote voluminously over the years in the *Annals* and elsewhere, presenting and explaining her teachings, her history, her customs, her treasures. He was offended by attacks on the Church and once said to me, 'If people would only take the time to get to know the Church, they could not help falling in love with her.' He did not like the idea of Catholics referring to themselves merely as Christians; they should be proud of their Catholic Faith.

Some, perhaps many, regarded Paul as a hard-line Catholic ideologue. But he understood the complexity of the human condition better than most and, while never casting principle aside, his approach to those in personal difficulties or in morally dubious circumstances was unfailingly pastoral and kind. He once commented to me, 'the Church has never condemned anyone for not living up to what it teaches; it has only condemned them for denying what it teaches'.

A couple of years before he died Paul told me over lunch in Berrima that when he was young, he had been diagnosed as having a degree of Asperger's syndrome. A great deal about Paul then fell into place for me, the social awkwardness that I had occasionally noticed over the years, things about him that I found very frustrating. The foregoing paean notwithstanding, Paul and I certainly had our moments. Aspects of his and my characters and personalities guaranteed flaming rows from time to time. Each of us was as impatient, proud, stubborn, defensive, and irascible as the other, and, rightly or wrongly, from time to time I considered Paul to be manipulative. Nevertheless, he was always the first to extend the olive branch and so our differences were always quickly patched up. Father Paul Stenhouse MSC was pure gift to me, and he was my closest friend.

The *Annals*, 1889–2019

Paul Stenhouse MSC

After *The Bulletin*, first published in January 1880, *Annals Australia* is one of the oldest continuously published magazines, and one of the best-known religious journals in the country. Published by the Missionaries of the Sacred Heart from Randwick, NSW until 1915, and then from the Sacred Heart Monastery, Kensington, NSW, its history is, in a sense, the history of the Catholic Church in Australia from 1889 onwards.

It reflects that history and through its wide, especially its country-wide, distribution, it established and maintained contact decade after decade, with isolated rural communities and alienated urban communities, in a way that many church personnel could not.

Someone less closely involved with the magazine would perhaps be better placed than be present writer, to assess the history of *Annals* and its role in the modern Church. However, until such an independent assessment can be made, the present editor's views may not be entirely without relevance or interest.

The Early Years

The first issue of *Annals* appeared in 1889—nine years after *The Bulletin*, hot off the presses of the *Freeman's Journal*, first hit the streets. *Annals* was merely one among dozens of literary, political and religious newspapers and journals that mushroomed in the Australia of the 70s and 80s in the 19th century.

Almost everyone who had something to say and could write, was either editing, publishing or writing for some new paper.

Australia on the eve of nationhood was an exciting place to be, and social political and religious issues were more on people's lips and pens than today.

Journalism then, (if I may quote an ex-editor of a popular mass circulation journal) wasn't as it appears to be now, at the service of an industry where clever marketing and quick returns totally outweigh truth and integrity.

Rather, in the 1880s, truth and integrity were catchcries fiercely, if at times inadvisedly, pursued: not a lot of thought was given to libel laws, so-called sacred cows, or others' feelings.

Readers of *The Bulletin*, with its well-known opposition to Asian migration, organised religion, female emancipation, and the monarchy (to mention but a few of the favourite targets of *The Bully's* editorial writers, cartoonists and bursa fires) would have been bemused, to say the least, by issues of *The Annals of Our Lady of the Sacred Heart* as it was then known.

No more bemused, perhaps, than the present *Annals* editor's own great-grandfather, John Farrell, poet, patriot and social reformer, his journalistic career was divided between various country newspapers he owned or edited. *The Bulletin*, to which he contributed verse from its earliest years, and the *Daily Telegraph* (or the '*Daily Twaddlegraph*' as it was irreverently referred to by *The Bulletin*) of which he was leader writer and at one time Editor.

Farrell, like many of his literary contemporaries, had little patience for clerical journals, and would not have approved of yet another religious voice being heard around Sydney.

Annals was modelled, in its content and design, on its old-world prototype, *Les Annales de Notre Dame du Sacre Coeur*. This latter was published from Issoudun, once a Roman camp, Eoldunum, but in the 1880s a sleepy little provincial town south of Bourges, in central France.

The original *Annals* had been the brainchild of Victor Jouet, MSC, a Corsican priest who could never have dreamed how successful his magazine, first established in 1866) could have become with a circulation in 1989 of well over 150,000 copies sold per month in France.

Editions had already (by 1889) appeared in Flemish, German, Spanish, Hungarian and American English, so the Australian addition wasn't unprecedented in the relatively short history of the Missionaries of the Sacred Heart.

An octavo-size monthly of 24 pages, costing two shillings annually or 2d an issue, *Annals* was printed by O'Hara and Johnson, 29 Jamieson Street Sydney. It had an elaborate engraving of Our Lady of the Sacred Heart on the front cover and with its exclusively Catholic news and hefty dose of mainly French piety—even down to citations from French bishops—and its interest in the mission to the natures of Papua New Guinea, Annals must have seemed anachronistic to the liberal minded Sydney *Bohemians*.

One of its most popular features was a regular serial, usually on a devout and edifying theme, that ran for years.

In time, *The Little Blue Book*, as it was to become known affectionately to generations of Catholic readers, often surpassed its sceptical and more cynical seniors in circulation, and won an assured place in the written, but largely unresearched history of Catholic journalism in Australia.

With one exception—the Jesuit *Messenger of the Sacred Heart*, first published in 1886—*Annals* alone of the many religious publications of the day has survived into this first quarter of the 21st-century.

Most of its secular contemporaries, too, although numerous and popular at the time, have returned to the pulp, lead and dust out of which they were produced. Even their names have been largely forgotten. How many today have even heard of, let alone mourn the passing, of *The Boomerang, The Illustrated Sydney News, The Picturesque Atlas of Australasia, the Australian Standard, The Lone Hand, The Stockwhip and Satirist, The Express, The Melbourne Star* or *The Sydney Evening News*?

The first editor of the *Annals of Our Lady of the Sacred Heart* was, surprisingly for the time, a woman.

Mary Agnes Finn, a devout member of an old-established Randwick Catholic family, was assisted by father Emile moved MSC, and Alsatian priest whose English at the time was poor and who was, on paper, responsible for the editing and production of the infant magazine.

Because of attitudes prevailing at the time, Mary Agnes Finn was never given the recognition that was heard you. Her role as editor was never publicised, and apart from the regular pieces carrying her by-line, she worked to relative obscurity. Yet her role was crucial.

The fairly immediate success of the new journal can be attributed to a number of factors, chief amongst which was the message of hope and love it carried to a Catholic community suffering greatly not just from the physical isolation of the Australian outback, but from the social and economic isolation that automatically followed from being a Catholic in an Anglo-Saxon and Protestant country.

Annals brought a world where other Catholics lived, closer to home, and lessened the loneliness and despair that often filled the slab hearts and below stairs accommodation that was 'home' to the over-idealised Irish mother.

Over the period 1889–1966, *Annals* was mainly mission-oriented, with special emphasis on Papua New Guinea and the Australian Aboriginal missions conducted by the Missionaries of the Sacred Heart, and because of this it is a unique resource for the religious and social historian.

This was its strength and the magazine reflected the strong self-image of the MSC over these years.

Not that the missions totally dominated the pages of the *Annals* in those years. Devotion to the Sacred Heart and to Our Lady of the Sacred Part was a feature, as were the serialised stories referred to above. After the First World War, *Annals* increased in size by eight pages, and the circulation increased as well. Some new features were added: the Question Box and the Children's Annals.

For a time, the Irish Question became a burning issue during the editorship of Father Michael Davitt Forest MSC who wrote under the pen name of The Wanderer. During these years, devotion to a newly canonised St, St Therese of Lisieux, occupied a prominent place in the magazine's Children's Page, and a new writer, Agatha le Bretton, who run who wrote under the pen name of Miriam Agatha, began to contribute short stories and cereals.

The Golden Age was probably during the late 1920s, when the magazine grew to 64 pages (but cost only one penny more an issue) and was printed on better quality paper, with a more professional approach to layout and design. The size of the pages was still octavo, but the quality of editing improved, especially under the editorship of Fathers Eric Dignan, Mortimer Kerrins and Thomas Ormond MSC, 1926–36. The latter increased the magazine's size from octavo to quarto and broadened the editorial outlook to include discussions of contemporary issues like the Spanish Civil War.

Internationally known Catholic writers contributed articles to *Annals* by arrangement with overseas journals. Maisie Ward, G.K. Chesterton, Hilaire Belloc, C.C. Martindale SJ all appeared from time to time in *Annals* as did local writers like Dame Mary Gilmore, Susan Gavin Duffy, Beatrice Grimshaw, Dr Leslie Rumble MSC, Dr Pat Ryan MSC and many others. Frank Sheed, founder of the Catholic publishing house Sheed and Ward made his debut as a writer in *Annals*.

The News service of the NCWC was a source of Catholic world news and Catholic Action as a subject was frequent and popular.

Annals *and Catechetics*

My first association with *Annals* dates from 1953, when an advertisement for the MSC Minor Seminary at St Mary's Towers, Douglas Park, New South Wales, caught the eye of a 17-year-old would-be linotypist/compositor/reporter working at the time for *The Camden News*.

Eleven years later, in 1964, I was appointed Business Manager of *Annals*, thus beginning a career with the magazine that apart from a five-year absence from 1977/1981, has covered 51 years.

At that time *Annals* was edited by Father Aloysius English MSC, aided by Mr John O'Loughlin of the Lewisham Printing firm. Father English continued the missionary and spiritual emphases of previous editors, adding his own 'light' touch through contributions he included on subjects that range from science (biology, botany, astronomy) to biography, theology, history, and (unusual for those days) school counselling and catechetics.

The trend away from 'religious' journalism in the narrowest sense of that word was really set by Father English's predecessor, Father Leo Dalton MSC and outstanding radio-broadcaster and a priest unusually gifted in English literature and language.

Numbers of subscribers had started to fall around this time, fluctuating around 30,000; although in its early days, *The Little Blue Book* boasted of a regular 45,000–50,000 monthly circulation.

By the time I became editor for the first time (in 1966) the circulation had settled at 25,000 monthly, and there were some who thought the *Annals* had had her day!

Certainly, TV, still at that time a relative novelty in Australia, and ever-present radio, had captured the market from magazines; pessimists were predicting that, before long, newspapers and books would be things of the past.

However wildly short of the mark that opinion may have proved to be, it can't be denied that the print industry was starting to reel under blows from its sister media, TV and radio. These inexorably attracted eyes and ears from the printed word, no matter how well written or designed, to the magic screen or radio enshrined in what was rather incongruously termed the morning MSC community 'living' room of most homes.

Could any magazine, aspiring even to modest editorial or topographical heights, hope to survive such onslaughts, when the mighty Cinema was closing down in suburb after suburb, and printing and postage costs were on the increase?

Advertising and at times overt exploitation of sexual and violent themes might keep certain kinds of backyard magazines still on the newsagents' shelves, but what future was therefore a religious magazine?

In 1967 the 'old lady', by then 78 years old, looking none the worse for wear (although a little piqued by reports that some readers to the north of Australia enjoyed *Annals* because the paper was excellent for rolling cigarettes!) shook her skirts and strode into the 70s.

The occasion of this rejuvenation was a chance attendance at a talk given by visiting Belgian writer on catechetics, Father Marcel Van Caster. Visiting Sydney and lecturing on religious education, Father Van Caster assured his listeners that all would be well in this next area when he and his colleagues in Europe finally unravelled the mysteries and made their conclusions available to a waiting world.

Some of us came away from that talk unconvinced that the promised help would arrive soon, but full of enthusiasm and interest in the urgent needs of Catholic parents and teachers for good, locally produced, catechetical material.

From that germ of an idea grew what was to become the major catechetical resource available in Australia to students in the top two years of secondary school for almost the next 10 years, namely: the *Annals* Catechetical Supplement, with

Teachers' Guide.

The first issue of *Annals* for 1968 carried a new name: *Annals '68*. The former name, *Annals of Our Lady of the Sacred Heart*, had not been dropped from any lack of regard for Our Lady whose magazine that remained, but from a sensitivity to the kind of language that young people were using in those days. If they were to be helped, then they would have to be attracted to read the material presented to them. And a magazine name that seemed to represent an older religious spirit to which they could not relate so easily at that time a fashionable student revolt, seemed to be an additional burden the newly redesigned magazine to carry.

This seemed especially valid in the light of the fact that the late 60s and early 70s were times of extraordinary social and political turmoil, with the so-called 'generation gap' ever widening. Religious and family life couldn't help but catch some of the flak that was thrown up by grass-roots unrest, nonetheless real for the difficulty most people—parents and children alike—found in articulating it.

The period 1968–74 was one of phenomenal success for *Annals* although it wasn't all plain sailing as anyone growing up at the time will remember.

Our confidence that underlying optimism and honesty of the youth of that difficult period would prevail over attempts to stifle its faith with 'God is Dead' slogans, the cult of drugs, pornography and revolt against all authority, no matter how moderate, was proven to be well-founded.

In the early decades of the *Annals* is chief supporters had been priests, nuns and laity who willingly undertook to distribute the magazine among Catholic people and thereby spread devotion to the Sacred Heart of Jesus and to Our Lady of the Sacred Heart along with it. This source of generous help in promoting *Annals* was drying up.

In the 60s most copies of *Annals* were distributed not through primary schools, as before, but through secondary schools and by their students to parents, most of whom lived by this time in cities and dormitory suburbs. Many of the topics that were to be discussed in *Annals* over the next 10 years or so, reflected the social pressures caused by the exodus from the country and the growing feeling of insecurity in a society whose Judeo-Christian foundations was starting to crumble or perhaps more correctly, to be whittled away.

Most Catholic secondary schools purchased large quantities of *Annals*. Many non-Catholic and even some State schools likewise received bulk copies for class use, or single copies for their libraries. Chaplains in non-Catholic schools also welcomed religious education material that was thoroughly Australian in content and design, and while non-polemical, was still unashamedly Catholic.

Month by month enough discussions and resource material was provided for a regular series of religion classes. The topics were selected from ones suggested by feed-back from readers, from *Annals* surveys carried out in schools in most states, and from ideas that were put forward by the Board that assisted the editor in the production of the Supplements. The topics were ones that Catholic adolescents were already discussing among themselves, and others that may not have been commonly discussed, but needed to be.

Annals in that first year offered material for class discussion on the following subjects: Friendship, Drug-taking, the search for meaning in life, the Race War, the Changing Church, War, Where are we heading?, Capital punishment, The Bible Today, Love.

Abortion was presented for the gruesome murder of helpless life that it is (and the *Annals* got publicly burned for its trouble) and future issues carried material on social justice, theology, history, morality, relationship questions relevant to adolescents at school, at play and at home, with their parents, their peers, and other adults, with authority figures in society, and their teachers, with the church. Sexual questions that were openly discussed on TV and radio were treated objectively and from a Catholic moral standpoint.

The circulation of *Annals* climbed steadily in these years, from 25,000 in 1966 to over 58,000 in 1972. Some months saw as many as 70,000 copies being sold.

As well as providing catechetical material for class use by students, a Teachers' Guide was produced every month. This offered advice on teaching methods, background readings, references to Church Fathers and documents as well as a suggested responses to the many questions that were raised in the students' Supplement, so as to ensure the teachers were helped to make the best possible use of the material.

Nothing was haphazard. At the beginning of the school year, parents, teachers and priests were notified of the course that *Annals* was planning to follow for the new year; and this plan was faithfully followed.

Material for the Supplements and the Teachers Guide was prepared by the editor; Boards, I quickly learned, may be an invaluable aid and be happy to comment on ideas or material already elaborated, but they usually too cumbersome to draw up material on a regular monthly basis for a magazine working to strict deadline.

* * *

When the history of religious education in Australia comes to be written, I have every confidence that the contribution of Annals will be seen to have been not inconsiderable.

Looking back on those years (1966–76), when is Editor of *Annals*, I was associated with many gifted priests and religious and laymen and women who were completely dedicated to the cause of communicating the faith post-Vatican to Catholic youth. I find myself echoing wholeheartedly the remark made years ago on French television by the then Archbishop of Paris, Cardinal Lustiger: 'we are only at the beginning of the Christian era, not at the end'. This was our firmly held conviction in the 60s and 70s. It still is, as we approach the third decade of the 21st-century.

The quest of religious educators then was not for novelty in doctrine, but for effective ways of making the old and perennial truths reach young people's hearts, and fuel their life systems, instead of remaining merely on the surface, to peel off in the heat of tension, or under pressure from temptation, or simply from the unexpected.

In these calmer days, it may be possible to say without reopening old wounds that for many older Catholics, the old ways were not entirely successful in providing them with the kinds of faith that could stand up to the rigours of survival in a deeply secularised and materialistic world.

Parents who longed, as many did, the beauty of the Latin liturgy, also looked forward to a return to the Penny

Catechism, and to the days when Catholic religious were numerous enough to staff our schools without having to employ others, were echoing the sentiments in many hearts during those years.

And when some refused to acknowledge as their son, a young man who refused on conscientious grounds to take an active part in (the Vietnam) war, it seemed to many of us that a certain perspective had become obscured and that sympathetic help was required for all concerned in these terrible human tragedies that were striking our Catholic people.

Many of us went in search of that key link in the chain of faith, that *elan vital* which makes faith come alive with God's spirit. We were all searching for something to lessen the heartache that many felt in the confusion of those days, and arrive at a method of presenting the faith for what it is—not just a series of formulae to which we assent with our minds, but a blueprint for life, that will touch our very being and sustain us through no matter what difficulties.

Whatever success *Annals* achieved in those difficult but tremendous years was due to the fact that *Annals* policy reflected an overall conviction among Missionaries of the Sacred Heart that the Catholic Faith had a supreme relevance for alienated men and women and youth; and that to filled a desperately felt need.

In 1977–81, I found myself in Rome as secretary to Father Jim Cuskelly, Superior General of the Missionaries of the Sacred Heart. My successor as editor of *Annals* was a friend, the gifted son and stepson of two outstanding Australian newsman. Geoff Baumgartner's father Charles, and his stepfather John

Waters, were both Editors of the *Melbourne Herald and Weekly Times*. Geoff continued the tradition establish for Annals in the 60s, but found that the context had changed in the intervening period. His editorship was a time of difficulties, but also one of reassessment.

Overseas catechesis had become acceptable in the Australia of the 80s in a way that would not have been possible in the 60s and 70s. This has been achieved chiefly through European and US trained Australian Religious Education teachers and catechists. And with this broadening of the catechetical perspective went a regularising of matter of religious syllabuses in Catholic Schools. By now each Catholic Diocese had its own RE program, unfortunately not always coordinated with the syllabuses used by other Dioceses. But the need for the *Annals* Syllabus was no longer so pressing.

As a result, the Teachers' Guide and Catechetical supplement ceased at the end of 1976, with my last issue, to be replaced by up-to-date courses in Scripture and theology, for students and parents alike.

By 1981 *Annals* was still useful and appreciated, but no longer indispensable; and voices were again raised suggesting that the now 92-year-old lady should be pensioned off.

Circulation had dropped dramatically and a rethinking of the role (if any) that a Catholic magazine could play in Australia at the 80s seemed called for.

Annals, *Journal of Catholic Culture*

With what I believe to have been a correct perception, *Annals* was, accordingly transformed in November-December 1981, into *Annals Australia: A Journal of Catholic Culture*, a vehicle for the transmission of Catholic Culture in all its diversity and richness.

Geoff Baumgartner graciously stepped down as editor, and I found myself editor of the re-designed *Annals* which was and is still aimed at families, at adult-education groups, and at the senior levels in secondary schools.

The need of the 80s and 90s, as I saw it, was for a rediscovery of our Catholic identity within a pluralistic society which gives no one marks for standing out or for being distinctive. And yet, the past, present and future forms of Catholicism are all inextricably bound together. To have an identity is to know where one comes from; to be someone is above all to stand somewhere!

Cult (worship of God) and culture are not simply similar sounding words. Culture in its fullest human sense is worshipful, and mindful of God. It embraces every aspect of our lives, and the reality of Catholic culture is as rich and varied as life itself. Exactly what Catholic culture is, and how it should be appreciated and passed on, is what *Annals Australia* sought to communicate.

This isn't all that different from what we have been trying to do for the past 130 years; only the emphasis has shifted and the magazine is aimed at a broader audience than secondary school students, although their faith growth is still our concern.

Following on the well-known statement, 'Christian is my first name; but Catholic is my family name', *Annals* was becoming more and more truly a family magazine; for the immediate family, but about the wider family which is universal (Catholic) by definition.

Catholicism is not a sect. People who try to turn us into a sect use terms like Roman Catholic which implies that we are simply not Church of England, Uniting Church, not Baptist, or Presbyterian, and so on. This is an impossible distortion of the Catholic identity and when people don't truly understand the nature of Catholicism, they naturally become confused and (if teachers or parents) confusing.

There is nothing limited about our Faith. We should be universal in our belief; in our acceptance of others, in our appreciation of the total picture. Partial reality, like partial truth, should be distasteful to us. We belong to the most culturally and linguistically diversified group in the world. We are heirs to traditions which, properly understood, would enrich not just our own lives, but the lives of all our fellow-citizens.

Annals Australia despite her 130 years, is still convinced that a sense of identity is crucial for survival in a society like ours which is dangerously paternalistic, accepting newcomers (and allcomers) on condition that they don't rock the boat, and that they blend comfortably into the all too often bland and anonymous background that we call Australian Society.

Too many Catholics these days look, sound and act just like everyone else. While this may make for comfortable living, it also leads to a loss of a sense of personhood with the resultant weakening of initiative and loss of freedom. If we have no past, or at least are unaware of it or disinterested in it, then we have no present let alone a future; and we're nobody!

To quote Cardinal Lustiger again, from his interview on French television to which I referred above:

I think that it is only in our day that humanity has really come face-to-face with itself: it is only now that we know all the peoples of the earth; we appreciate only now the terrifying and fascinating power and capability of human intellect, it is only now that the human race has articulated certain moral problems to which Christianity alone is able to give an answer.

That and some cannot be given in or from a vacuum. To be able to respond as we should, to the deepest cries of humankind, Catholics must know who they are, and where they have come from.

In 1989, after eight years of being produced in its present form, *Annals* built up a circulation of 20,000, most of which went to homes around Sydney, and especially in the Eastern Suburbs, though all Australian states were represented in our database. The response of Australian Catholics to the as-yet limited promotion was encouraging.

The second issue of 1889 cost only 3d. Thirty-six years later, in 1925, one shilling, in 1966, $0.4 (equivalent to 4 shillings) and in 1976, but one dollar (equivalent to 10 shillings), in 1984, and $2. six years later in 1990! We have kept the price at $3 (plus 30 cents GST) since 1999 when we had to praise the price to $3 and in the millennium year 2000, GST was applied.

The problems facing and magazines like *Annals*, and indeed every newspaper and journal that cannot afford to be distributed through the newsagents, are enormous. In 1989, to send one bill to 20,000 subscribers cost $8200 simply for the postage stamps required! In 2019 it would cost $20,000. So billing subscribers became a grave financial burden, and other ways had to be found to encourage readers to re-subscribe voluntarily.

Even some Catholic firms hesitated to advertise in Catholic newspapers and journals often for the very good reason that the typographical and journalistic standards are simply not high enough, but sometimes also out of a reluctance to be associated with a religious journal for fear that all religious journals will approach them for advertising!

Fortunately over the years, *Annals* has been supported by numerous advertisers whose wares and services *Annals* has been happy to recommend to subscribers.

Annals has always found that an unwillingness to compromise in matters of sound typography enhances the effectiveness of the magazine. We will never forget Hal English, whose superb, I'm tempted to say unique, artistic talent, all self-taught, he shared with us, month after month, from 1981 until his death in 1986. And after Hal, Cliff Baxter, an old newspaperman friend of years ago, introduced us to Kevin Drumm, who became our caricaturist for many years, and died in 2006, and is still much missed. In what now seems the remote past, in the 60s and 70s, how then printers, O'Loughlin Bros of Lewisham, would regularly win prizes for their printing of *Annals*, the Sydney Royal Easter show.

In 1989, I wrote in *Annals*,

> What the future holds for *Annals Australia* remains to be spelt out. However, I am convinced that it continues to have a critical role to play in the growth in cultural self-awareness of Australian Catholics. To have done useful work in the past is, I know, no reason for being confident that a magazine will still flourish in a world that is aeons away from the one into which it was born.

But to have helped mould that future world, to have promoted a love for what is true, good and beautiful in our Catholic heritage, carries with it a certain confidence that *Annals* will survive to be read by future generations of Australian Catholics.

Sadly, owing to circumstances touched on above, this will be the final issue of *Annals Australasia*. That she survived into her 130th year is a tribute to all of you, our faithful subscribers, benefactors, and to members of our MSC Provincial Councils down the years.

In a poem of Dame Mary's, 'By the Roadside', printed for the first time in *Annals* (December 1926) we can find a crystallising of the aims of this most Australian Catholic Magazines:

Wonder is dead, you say!/ Wonder can never die.
Not while within a shining pool/ A man can see the sky.

It is as a shining pool reflecting the wonders of God and his creation that *Annals* should be remembered. Age could do little to mark the image that it reflects.

Kensington, New South Wales, November 29, 2019.

[Paul died on November 19 and was buried on November 27. A summary of this article which appeared in Annals 2019/9, was read at a commemorative lunch for Annals at Sacred Heart Monastery, Kensington, by Michael Wilding. It was attended by Paul's family, many contributors to Annals, and Missionaries of the Sacred Heart.]

PART II

PRIEST-SCHOLAR

Karl Schmude

Paul Stenhouse MSC was an unconventional scholar-priest. He was immensely erudite but did not parade his learning or allow it to distance him, as a priest, from those who were less learned. He took part in scholarly research and discussion and enjoyed strong academic friendships (such as with James Waldersee, Pierre Ryckmans and Michael Wilding), while believing that scholarship should serve the needs of wider communities and not be confined to the enlightenment of fellow scholars. He was a brilliant linguist, proficient in many languages, but could speak in plain words to various audiences—as a priest, to church congregations; as a foreign journalist, to Australian readers; as a Catholic writer and editor, to dedicated subscribers. He was a gifted teacher, clear and compelling, though not a regular lecturer. He was a skilled translator and interpreter of historical, at times esoteric, texts, but was especially recognised for his presentation of learning in popular media—a daily newspaper such as The Australian, and above all the monthly journal, Annals.

I came to know Paul Stenhouse in the 1970s when he began publishing articles I had written on Catholic authors, notably G. K. Chesterton and Christopher Dawson. I soon realised that his life was a deep integration of the natural and the supernatural—of accumulated wisdom and consecrated love. He fitted Pascal's succinct description of intellectual prowess and spiritual fidelity perfectly: 'Pious scholars rare.'[1]

He was, first and foremost, a priest who took scholarly learning seriously, not a scholar who took the priesthood seriously. In an era when religious faith is discounted by the assumed superiority of academic or scientific knowledge, Paul had a clear sense of vocational primacy. He recognised the spiritual and intellectual riches that come from learning based on reason and research, but he understood that these are deepened, not demeaned, when harmonised with the insights of divine revelation. He knew the power of incarnated reality—the human stories and higher symbols of baptised history, which invest human life with transcendental purpose and significance.

Paul's life of learning and culture had strong family roots. His great grandfather in 19th century Australia was John Farrell, who combined the flair of a reforming journalist and editor with a poetic sensibility. Farrell offered an early intimation of Paul's distinctive fusion of cultural intelligence and editorial imagination.[2] In a more direct and personal sense, these and other qualities were fostered from his early childhood. His mother stimulated his interest in words. She had a love of languages, both European and Middle-Eastern, extending, on the one hand, to Latin, Italian, Spanish and French, and on the other, to Arabic as a result of connections with a Maronite family in Sydney. His mother's influence was far-reaching—stemming, in the words of his fellow MSC priest, John McMahon, from 'her many gifts of mind and spirit.'[3]

His family education in languages was the foundation of an extended linguistic and intellectual formation. In 1968 he embarked upon a Bachelor of Arts degree at the University of Sydney. It culminated in his graduating with Honours in 1972, majoring in Modern Hebrew and Arabic languages. His Honours thesis, titled 'A Critical Edition of the historical sections of the Samaritan Hebrew Hilukh,' led to further studies in Arabic and Samaritan.

By this time Paul had developed a deep fascination with Samaritan history and culture and its connections with the faith of the Old Testament. He realised, as he later recalled, that there was 'Samaritan Arabic, just as there is a special kind of Christian Arabic and Jewish Arabic.'[4] He then enrolled in an Honours Master of Arts at the University of Sydney, intending to translate and comment on the Arabic 'History of the Samaritans' of Abu'l-Fath, a 14th century Samaritan who chronicled the history of his Palestine-based people from Adam to Mohammed.

This proved to be a formidable undertaking. The manuscript for the history had become so corrupted that translating the work of the Samaritan chronicler involved interpreting and reconciling about thirty or so original manuscripts. A critical edition based on those manuscripts was required, not simply a translation. Thus Paul's MA thesis was elevated to a PhD dissertation.

However, in 1976, he embarked on a different course of

studies. Instead of completing his degree in Sydney, he left Annals, which he had been editing for ten years (1966–76), and enrolled in a Doctor of Philosophy (DPhil) at St Catherine's College, Oxford. This plan did not finally materialise. On his way to Rome he responded to a call to serve for the next three years as private secretary to the Australian superior-general of his Order, Father (later Bishop) E.J. Cuskelly MSC.

In 1979, Paul left Rome for Yugoslavia to work on the various manuscripts he had brought with him to Europe. A priest-friend offered him a dilapidated seminary in the city of Sarajevo as a quiet place for research. Paul found this a congenial refuge and enjoyed the discovery of many Arab manuscripts in the nearby mosques. But shortly afterwards, he was expelled by the military police for being a Catholic priest—who was, moreover, from Australia—and he 'was exiled to Dubrovnik.'[5] He stayed happily in this port city on the Dalmatian Coast for almost a year, completing his dissertation in three volumes, and subsequently receiving his PhD from the University of Sydney.[6] As he later showed in his promotion of the work in many countries of the Catholic charity, Aid to the Church in Need, he did not need to be a parish priest. The world was his parish.

The troubled history of his doctoral studies revealed the distinctive qualities of Paul's life as a scholar-priest—a dynamic blend of esoteric learning and earthly enterprise. From his first university days, he realised that he was 'very much at the pit face,'[7] mastering the languages of an ancient Semitic world while being immersed in the cauldron of present-day Middle East politics. The study of ancient religious texts carried an unavoidable contemporary relevance for him. It afforded a profound perspective on the trouble spots of his time attuned as he was to the Middle East and the Balkans with their perpetual entanglements of religion and politics. Not for nothing did he have a scholarly grounding in ancient Samaria, a land that had now assumed a painfully modern expression in the disputed territory of the West Bank.

In the Lebanese Civil War (1975–90), he made frequent visits to Beirut as a foreign correspondent. He wrote authoritative pieces for *The Australian* and the *Courier-Mail*, as well as for Italian and Arabic newspapers. The experience also revealed his deeply practical acumen and readiness to take risks in the cause of good. On one occasion he hired a boat in Malta and smuggled medicine, donated by Australian pharmaceutical companies, to needy peoples in the lands of the Levant. It was unauthorised and audacious, and it overcame the previous failures through official channels, where aid ended up in the hands of bandits and militias.[8]

Paul's academic expertise in Semitic languages could easily have justified an academic career, but he believed this would have been at odds with his priestly vocation. 'I was invited to teach Middle Arabic once,' he recalled in one interview, 'but I didn't accept, because there are so few people willing to learn it that for a priest to be spending his life doing that didn't make much sense.'[9]

For a time at Sydney University he taught a course of greater breadth and student interest, focusing on various aspects of the period between the Old and New Testaments.[10] But his desire to teach took a different form and reached out to a larger audience. He placed his scholarship at the service of the Church and made available the bountiful fruits of his learning to the subscribers of *Annals*, as well as to a general readership as a mainstream journalist.

Through his work as a scholar-priest, Annals embodied a special blend of qualities. It was scholarly, in making known the best learning in such areas as history, literature, philosophy and theology. It was visually impressive, displaying the evocative work of artists such as Hal English, and drawing on Paul's skill as a photographer who could capture pictures that illustrated the incarnational character of the Christian faith. And it was Catholic, in presenting unambiguously the teachings and traditions of the Church; in particular, the abundance of their cultural expression.

While the journal's title changed over the 130 years of its publication, from the explicitly devotional *Annals of Our Lady of the Sacred Heart* to the more general *Annals Australia*, and finally *Annals Australasia*, Paul added in 1981 the sub-title, 'Journal of Catholic Culture'. This did not reflect a narrowing of vision or a new denominational focus, but was simply to affirm with St Pacianus of Barcelona, who died in AD391: 'Christianus mihi nomen est, Catholicus vero cognomen— Christian is my first name, but my surname is Catholic'.[11] The sub-title also emphasised the journal's educational and evangelising purpose in an Australian—and more broadly Western—culture that was rapidly jettisoning its Christian heritage and emptying out its religious memory.

A significant, if modest, example of Paul's efforts to respond to this religious and cultural amnesia with accessible and appealing learning was his publication in 1992 of *Annals Almanac of Catholic Curiosities*. In the Preface, he hoped that all those who dipped into its myriad stories and memories would find 'their hearts lightened, and their minds enlightened.' He invoked the maternal image of the Church which he always loved:

> Like a true mother, she honours history, but loves and respects legends and folklore. She knows that tradition is the lifeline that ties our faith to its origins and enables us to move confidently into the future. She is patient with her impatient children, continuing to love them in her ever-young hope that they will eventually recognise whose love is truest.[12]

Paul's abiding mission was apostolic. In looking back on his remarkably long editorship of *Annals*—from 1966 until his death in 2019, with a hiatus of five years between 1976 and 1981 when he was overseas—his deep sense of the integrity and continuity of the journal is unmistakable, adjusted as it needed to be to the challenges of new circumstances:

> I have tried to keep Our Lady to the forefront to the best I can in a way which is in keeping with the modern times in which we live. I have also tried to keep the Annals as a vehicle for spreading and defending the faith as fearlessly as I can, and to a certain extent it is a bit of a lone voice. There are other journals around, but they are all different from the Annals.[13]

They were 'all different' because Paul Stenhouse was 'all different'.

A fundamental part of that difference can be found in the intellectual framework of his editorship, which might be a synthesis of learning in the light of Catholic faith and tradition, and it animated every issue of *Annals*. When he discovered that this heritage would form the core teaching program of a proposed Catholic institution, Campion College Australia, he was ardent in his support. He publicised in *Annals* the development of the College and contributed to a Campion publication an early article on the nature of the Catholic liberal arts, under the title, 'An intellectual and creative home for the searching heart'.[14] He served on the College's governing board in the early years, and arranged for its meetings to take place at the MSC Monastery in Kensington before it found a campus in the western Sydney suburb of Toongabbie where it opened in 2006.

At a celebration of the 25th anniversary of his priesthood, Paul spoke of the supreme challenge of being a Catholic and a Catholic priest:

> It tenses one's every muscle and drains every nervous cell in one's body as [the Church] endeavours to pass on to us the torch of unwritten and written tradition handed down through the past 2000 years. Some of us fumble a lot, some of us even momentarily drop the torch, but I hope that its light is burning no less brightly for having been in my hands.[15]

Paul's hope is one that we can confidently cherish, as we recall with gratitude the ways in which he illuminated so many lives with the torch he faithfully carried throughout his long life as a scholar-priest.

Notes

1. Pensée 956, in Pensées / Pascal; trans. with an introduction by A.J. Krailsheimer (London, UK: Penguin Books, 1995), p. 329.

2. The range and depth of John Farrell's influence are clear from Paul Stenhouse's biography, which began as an Honours/ Masters thesis at the University of New England, *John Farrell: Poet, Journalist and Social Reformer, 1851–1904* (North Melbourne: Australian Scholarly Publishing, 2018).

3. John F. McMahon, 'About the Editor,' *Annals Australia*, June 1988, p.44. I am indebted to Fr McMahon's article for many of the background details on Paul that are included in this chapter.

4. Chris Lindsay, "'Secret agenda' gave way to Middle East studies,' *Catholic Weekly* (Sydney), January 9, 2005, p. 23.

5. Chris Lindsay, ibid.

6. The dissertation was published in 1985 by the Mandelbaum Trust at the University of Sydney under the title, The Kitab al-Tarikh of Abu l-Fath. It was listed as 'translated into English with notes by Paul Stenhouse', and was the first in the published series, *Studies in Judaica* (Sydney, NSW).

7. Chris Lindsay, ibid.

8. Marek Jan Chodakiewicz, 'Fr Paul Stenhouse, R.I.P.,' *Crisis Magazine*, January 21, 2020.

9. Chris Lindsay, ibid.

10. Chris Lindsay, ibid.

11. The Latin quotation came from St Pacianus' First Letter to Sympronianus Novatianus, De Catholico nomine, Jacques Paul Migne, Patres Latini, tome xiii, 1045ff. It was quoted in a brief

history of *Annals* at the beginning of its final year of publication in 2019: Paul Stenhouse, '*Annals Australasia, 1889–2019*,' *Annals Australasia*, January–February 2019, p. 3.

12. Paul Stenhouse MSC, *Annals Almanac of Catholic Curiosities* (Kensington, NSW: Chevalier Press, 1992).

13. Chris Lindsay, 'A Mission to spread, defend Catholic faith,' *Catholic Weekly* (Sydney), October 31, 2004, p. 9.

14. *Campion's Brag: Catholic Learning in the Liberal Arts*, Vol. 4, No. 4, Spring 2005, 4.

15. Cliff Baxter, 'Hundreds turn out for the 'priest of the Arabian Nights',' *Catholic Weekly* (Sydney), August 17, 1988, p. 12.

Extraordinary Scholar, Writer, and Witness to Eternity

Wanda Skowronska

I remember reading the Annals as a high school student. Never, ever, did I imagine that years later I would meet Fr Stenhouse one day and would be co-opted into that wide group writing for *Annals Australasia* (originally called *The Annals of Our Lady of the Sacred Heart*) for over 15 years. The *Annals*, as it is popularly known, was to become the longest-lived journal in Australian history, having been established here in 1889, continuing from its inception in France. It is great part of the history of the Missionaries of the Sacred Heart (MSCs) in this country, and I feel so privileged to have been a small part of it.

Shortly after his ordination, Fr Stenhouse took on the reins of Annals, after the expert editorship of Fr Aloysius English. Given his previous experience as a journalist, Fr Stenhouse was appointed as business manager of Annals in 1964 and editor in 1966, turbulent, post-war, post Vatican II times.

The journal became a transmitter of contemporary concerns, moral issues, catechesis, along with articles on history, literature, philosophy, films, music and language. While Fr Stenhouse had a wide knowledge of all these fields, when I met him, he conveyed a distinct air of being suspicious of psychology. Well, he would not have been the first to do so. He asked me a question along the lines of: 'So what makes you so sane?' Of course, I felt nonplussed and thought this was my cue to walk around the room like Inspector Clouseau in witty riposte. Instead I said that if you came from a family whose members had been in concentration camps and gulags, who had been shot, and tortured, you became inclined to have few illusions about humanity and to seek reality. He seemed to like that reply. And from that grew an invitation to write several articles on psychology. In this way I could write about what fascinated me, the cultural context of modern psychology, various current psychological concerns, and critiques of Freud, Jung and Rogers. I tried to be helpful in writing on the nature of autism, ADHD, and personality disorders, knowing how much they afflict the sufferer and those around them. I even wrote an article on link between psychology and exorcism and described, in Annals, an exorcism conference in Sydney, which I had attended at the invitation of Archbishop Julian Porteous.

Fr Stenhouse impressed many people with his knowledge of other cultures. I told him one day about Bonegilla, a migrant camp in northern Victoria, which few people seemed to know about. Fr Stenhouse knew where it was, its place in Australian history and in a very short time, I experienced that sense of someone 'getting it'. He could take on long and strange Polish, Ukrainian, Hungarian and Latvian names and recount stories of many unusual places. He gave the impression that he was genuinely interested in the whole world and he truly was.

Those who came to see Fr Stenhouse on various matters would recall walking into his office, with its ceiling to floor bookshelves and highly organised desk, with quotations affixed to it as well as many sticky note reminders. He always seemed to be extraordinarily busy with his research, writing, pastoral work, and continual phone calls—from anywhere in the world. One day, on entering this legendary office I found him poring over a manuscript with his finger going rapidly from right to left. I could see that the writing was in Arabic and I asked if he were reading something interesting and he said 'yes' in a very studious way. I imagine I had distracted him from some very interesting point. Fr Stenhouse could not only speak Arabic but he spoke it well (other Arabic speakers said so). He could say names like 'Abd-al-Aziz ibn Abd-Allah ibn Baaz' at the drop of a hat and could speak several Samaritan dialects including medieval Samaritan Arabic. He had studied Latin, Greek, Hebrew, Arabic, Syriac, Samaritan, Armenian and Ugaritic and could pray in Aramaic. He had done pioneering translations and research and was a member of the Société d'Études Samaritaines within the Collège de France (a prestigious higher education and research establishment founded in 1530). But such was his graciousness, that he put aside the papers to answer the questions I had for some article I was working on. He was kind in that way too many people from varied walks of life—from politicians, scholars, students and writers to the homeless and desperate who turned to him for help. A friend of his related that he was with Fr Stenhouse in the city once and it was pouring with rain. Fr Stenhouse saw an elderly lady getting drenched and he had no hesitation in going over to hold his umbrella above her, helped her walk to a taxi stand, hailed one for her and helped her inside. Such behaviour seemed to come from some deep well of kindness and courtesy that was as much a part of his nature as his intense intellectual pursuits. Fr Stenhouse truly followed the ideals exhorted of each missionary of the Sacred Heart, on the MSC website in the following words:

> It is necessary then that he shows forth in his life the great virtues of which Christ has left us such sublime examples. Like Christ, he should be meek and humble of heart; like Him, the priest should love poverty, practice penance, be sympathetic to the weak, be helpful to sinners and bring back the lost sheep on his shoulders to the divine fold. Like his Divine Model, the priest should be ready to suffer all things for the salvation of souls.[1]

Fr Stenhouse certainly spared himself no pains in helping those who suffered persecution for their faith, nor did he hesitate to build bridges with those of other cultures. He was such an intrepid traveller to far flung places, as *Annals* readers would recall. If you followed his travels, you could find him in Armenia interviewing refugees from Nagorno-Karabakh, interviewing Islamic Muftis in war-torn Syria, staying at the Topkapi Palace in Istanbul, deciphering inscriptions on walls in Kashmir, climbing mountains in China, or visiting Timbuktu. Yes, he really did visit Timbuktu and remarked that he found not one Catholic there. No doubt he said Mass as he passed though, though this would have been at considerable risk to himself.

In following those who were persecuted, he particularly monitored the fate of the eastern European Catholics during and after the Soviet era. He remarked in sombre tone:

> As the West stands back in wonder at the miraculous transformation of the former Communist states in the Baltic, Central and Eastern Europe, it would do well

to remember the millions of martyrs whose blood sowed the seeds that put down deep roots and today are budding and tomorrow will burst into flower. We can mention but a handful ... In June [1947] Archbishop Mecys Reinys, of Vilnius 'disappeared' after he was interviewed by a correspondent of the Tass newsagency. In July the nonagenarian Bishop Antonas Karosas of Seinai died, and not long afterwards, the sole remaining Bishop, Kazys Paltarokas of Penevezys, 'disappeared'.[2]

When he went to the Ukraine in 1991 with director Phillip Collignon, then director of Aid to the Church in Need, to witness the return of Myroslav Ivan Lubachivskyj, Great Archbishop of Lviv and Metropolitan of Galicia to his church once again, Fr Stenhouse was at one with the rejoicing throngs. He jumped on top of media vans to get good shots, talked to ordinary Ukrainians in the crowds, conversed with journalists, dined with Communists and the Archbishop himself, saying Mass with his Ukrainian brother priests after years of Soviet suffering.[3] In his *Annals* report on this, Fr Stenhouse gave a quick overview of the facts, characteristic of his extraordinary summaries of complex situations, saying so much in a single paragraph:

Myroslav Ivan Lubachivskyj was coming home after 52 years. He is the first Catholic Metropolitan Archbishop of Galicia to set foot in Lviv since April 11, 1945 when Metropolitan (later Cardinal) Josef Slipj was imprisoned, along with the entire Episcopate, 1735 priests, 1090 nuns and tens of thousands of lay Catholics. All the Ukrainian Byzantine Catholic bishops died in prison except Josef Slipj who paid for his refusal to convert to Russian Orthodoxy with a further seven years in prison and exile to Siberia. He was freed only in 1963 after the intervention of Pope John XXIII.[4]

Meticulous with historical detail, Fr Stenhouse gave eyewitness accounts so all could share his journeys. When he lived in Dubrovnik for several years, he got to know Croatian, and visited Slovenia and Albania, saying Masses in all those places where the Catholic church had suffered horrendously under the Communists. He travelled to Lebanon many times with his friend Joseph Assaf, climbing mountains with him, visiting Maronite enclaves, saying Masses in small churches, coming to love this country that had preserved the Catholic faith in the face of such long persecution.

Making contacts with many groups—Fr Stenhouse was a friend to Ukrainians, Poles, Lebanese, Syrians, Italians, Indonesians, Malaysians, and Vietnamese among others. Hendrikus Wong, a friend of Indonesian background, who helped him with computer matters and whom Fr Stenhouse helped in many ways, said he felt he owed his priest friend a great debt of gratitude. Fr Stenhouse reached out, helped many overseas students and became 'family' to those be befriended, visiting them in turn, in their countries. This reaching out extended to Jewish and Muslim groups. He regularly visited Jewish Professor Alan Crown who not only taught him Hebrew at Sydney University, but also medieval Samaritan. Professor Crown ended up writing several articles for *Annals*. In 2011, when Fr Stenhouse went to Damascus, he comforted a Sunni Muslim Mufti who had lost his son in war—for he had no trouble seeing our common humanity across many divides and had the gift of engendering trust. In speaking with the Mufti Muhammad Badr Din Hassoun in Arabic for several hours he was able to confirm that the Sunnis within Syria had not sought this war—it had come from external influences. As well as being an outstanding eye-witness account in Annals, this report made it into many mainstream media outlets, including *The Australian*.

Much more will come out in future years about the extraordinary life of this priest. Hopefully, students will have access to and consult the marvellous archives at the Monastery of the Sacred Heart, as well as the online Annals Archive, to pursue research on the myriad of topics Fr Stenhouse wrote about.[5] *Annals* is a student's treasure trove—there are several thesis topics buried in those archives!

Fr Stenhouse held up a torchlight of reason and faith in turbulent times and growing hostility to Christianity. He saw the various forms of cultural decay around him but did not yield to them, knowing that all on earth have it inscribed in their hearts and minds to seek meaning. He had a way of drawing people to him, talking on any topic under the sun, reflecting on events in the church with reason, knowledge and tranquillity and conveying all this to us in an extraordinary publication that lasted till just before he died on 19 November 2020. He gave a public lecture at Campion College a month before he died, with some subtle Chestertonian wit. He was the catalyst for many conversions to Catholicism and could converse at length with ex-Communist Rupert Lockwood, and even got him to write for *Annals*. Fanatics lost hope in his presence, unsound generalisations were taken apart by his scathing remarks, and spin was skewered by his pungent wit.

It was always the ideas he tore apart, never the person. The great legacy he bequeathed us all was his unswerving focus on seeking truth with equanimity.

He could truly be numbered among the 'blessed ... who find wisdom, those who gain understanding' (Proverbs 3:13). He shared this wisdom and understanding with all he met in a very humble way. He never hesitated to thread the visible world with divine realities and stood as a continual witness to them. In the end, all that he did was directed by his love for Christ, the church in its richness, suffering, history and grandeur.

1.From a website outlining the vision of Jules Chevalier, founder of the Missionaries of the Sacred Heart. 'Chevalier and his family':

http://www.sacredheart.org.au/nationalshrineOLSH/ Chevalier%20and%20Family.htm#spititualityoffatherfounder

2. Paul Stenhouse, 'Lest We Forget', *Annals Australasia*, July, 1990.

3. As told to me by Phillip Collignon, former Australian director of Aid to the Church in Need, who accompanied Fr Stenhouse to the Ukraine and witnessed these events.

4. Paul Stenhouse, 'CHRIST IS TRULY RISEN: The return of Great Archbishop Cardinal Myroslav Lubachivskyj to his faithful Byzantine-Rite Catholics', *Annals Australasia*, May, 1991.

https://web.archive.org/web/20150907145939/http://jloughnan. tripod.com/lestforget.htm

5. This online Archive can be found on:

https://web.archive.org/web/20151013181726/http://jloughnan. tripod.com/portal.htm#112

GOOD POLYMATH...GOOD PASTORAL PRIEST

Greg Sheridan

Greg Sheridan, the long-serving Foreign Affairs editor of The Australian newspaper, described Fr Stenhouse as much more than a friend. His tribute appeared in the Catholic Weekly, December 5th 2019.

Paul Stenhouse was a gifted polymath, a cosmopolite of astonishing diversity and virtuosity, a prodigious reader, a knower of infinite facts and theories, and a deeply wise, friendly, good, pastoral priest. Surprising as it may seem, that combination is not quite as common as you might think.

Paul was a friend of mine, but I was very slack about maintaining the friendship properly. Because he was so affable and easy going, and because I suffer from that tendency which besets many journalists to get in touch with friends when I need their help, my contact with him was spasmodic.

As a priest, he officiated at my wedding, helped me when I was sick, offered wise counsel more than once.

A respected public intellectual

But I also shamelessly drew on him as a great public intellectual, and talked to him about Islam, Indonesia, the Balkans, Lebanon, the Middle East more widely, medieval

Christianity, contemporary Christianity and any other subject which from time to time I needed input on.

I met him through another great polymath, the former Labor cabinet minister John Wheeldon. John was the associate editor of *The Australian* when I joined the paper in 1984. Although a conscientious atheist, John had the greatest admiration for Paul and the two were firm friends, although they tended to show off a bit in my company by speaking to each other in a variety of languages which I couldn't understand.

Paul befriended many journalists. He combined with his great learning a deep, priestly, pastoral personality, an ever friendly and cheerful demeanour and loads of common sense. My only difficult encounter with him came many years ago when I gave a lecture to a small group on Islam in Indonesia. Paul rose to ask a question. He lavished my feeble remarks with unjustified praise and then, politely and kindly, took them apart piece by piece.

And here is his true genius. I liked him just as much afterwards as before, and while I was perhaps none the wiser for the encounter, I was certainly better informed.'

Because of his (entirely justified) skepticism of the state of contemporary Australian tertiary education and because of the importance he saw in creating an answer, helping to establish and then promote Campion College, Australia's first Liberal Arts tertiary institution, became a personal mission.

ISLAM

Tony Abbott

Review, The Spectator, *21 December 2019, Islam: Context and Complexity, Pamphleteer (Australian Scholarly Publishing) 2019, 186pp. with footnotes.*

This easy-to-read volume of essays, each originally published in the journal of Catholic culture, *Annals Australasia*, is an important caveat to the simplistic notion that Islam is a religion of peace and that Islamist terrorists are not 'true Muslims'. For more than half a century, the author, a priest, has been a close student of Islam and the cultures of the Middle East, and has published translations of Arab history plus monographs on Middle Arabic. Few Australians have been more deeply intellectually immersed in Middle Eastern Muslim culture and are more qualified to assess political Islam and then explain it to a wider public.

Father Paul Stenhouse is profoundly sympathetic to those Muslims trying to redeem their faith from the grip of 'death to the infidel' theology, but far from certain that this humane re-interpretation is likely to prevail without much upheaval first. In part, this is because of the clumsiness of Western diplomacy that makes common cause with extremists, such as the Afghan Mujahideen, for instance, for immediate advantage against Soviet Russia, only to spawn al-Qaeda in the longer term. His book is a plea for greater understanding of the diversity of

Islam, as well as for caution in imagining that there can be Western-driven change for the better any time soon.

It goes almost without saying that most contemporary commentary on Islamist terrorism assumes that the West must really be to blame for it. Stenhouse is trenchantly critical of recent Western policy in Iraq, Afghanistan, Libya and Syria (somewhat too critical, in my view) but squarely faces the historical truth that Islam has almost always spread by conquest and that the overwhelmingly dominant strains of Islam (even now) see no separation between religion and politics and have no concept of minority rights.

Muslim rage, he points out, has almost nothing to do with the crusades, which only began half a millennium after Jerusalem was first lost to the Muslims. After 400 years of supposedly 'peaceful' coexistence between Christians and their Muslim rulers, the 700 Catholic bishops of North Africa had been reduced to just five by 1050. Mohammed might well have been, to the Muslim faithful, the prophet of God; but it was by military conquest that he established his authority. It was clearly laid down in his lifetime that the alternative to converting to Islam (which means 'submission' in Arabic) was death, or permanent subservience plus the payment of higher taxes. It's probably true that, in some instances, the peoples subject to Muslim invasion preferred Islamic conquest to the sometimes even more brutal and despotic Byzantine and Persian regimes of the time; nonetheless, within a century of Mohammed's death, the sword had carried Islam beyond the Pyrenees and to the gates of Constantinople.

Charles Martel may have beaten back the Moorish armies at Tours in southern France in 732 but for another three centuries, until the beginning of the crusades in the 11th century, Italy was subject to raids and partial Muslim conquest; and a Turkish army laid siege to Vienna as late as 1683. Irredentist Islamist leaders, such as Turkey's 'new sultan', Recep Erdogan, have forgotten none of this even if almost every Westerner has.

As Stenhouse sees it, the problem is the disconnect between the Mohammed of Mecca, who was the genial prophet of persuasion; and the Mohammed of Medina—the place to which he subsequently fled after a dispute—who was the militant prophet of compulsion. Unfortunately for subsequent history, all of Mohammed's recorded sayings are the inspired word of God; and the later Medina period has set the tone for all that's followed. If you like, it's the reverse of Christianity, where a later and much-more-genial New Testament supplemented and often enough supplanted the unforgiving Old one. As well, especially for the majority Sunni Muslims, there's no interpretive authority, equivalent to the Pope, or even the Archbishop of Canterbury, who can rule conclusively on which parts of the Muslim scripture apply literally, and which only figuratively to the modern world.

Stenhouse is an admirer of Mohamed Taha, a former imam in Omdurman and Muslim reformer, who said that the irenic Meccan texts should now take priority over the harsher Medina ones that had served their purpose. For drawing this distinction, he was executed in 1985. This is the fate of almost everyone who dares to question, in a Muslim country, the 'death to the infidel' orthodoxy that's generally accepted even by peaceful Muslims who wouldn't dream themselves of killing in the name of God.

In Stenhouse's judgment, the best that can be said of Islam is not that 'death to the infidel' is contrary to Muslim teaching; just that it's not commanded by it: hence the falsehood, repeatedly asserted by Western leaders, invariably after the latest atrocity, that Islam is really a 'religion of peace'. It may be a religion of peace, but it is certainly not necessarily so; and those Muslims who assert that it is, indeed, a religion of peace, at least in the Middle East, are at serious risk of being killed by their co-religionists. To Stenhouse, it is the duty of thoughtful Muslims, in relatively safe countries such as Australia, to do everything they can to cleanse Islam of violence; and it's the duty of the rest of us to give them every reasonable encouragement.

Father Stenhouse died last month, just a few weeks after this book was published, and a few days after he'd prepared what would turn out to be the last issue of *Annals*, the magazine he'd edited since 1964. Writers die, but their writings never do; and while they continue to be read the writer lives on, at least in spirit. After three decades of friendship, I owed him this review; to encourage others to get to know, albeit posthumously, a wonderful man, a fine teacher, and a friend of *The Spectator Australia.*

Islam

Piers Paul Read

Review: Islam. Context and Complexity. *Pamphleteer.*
Australian Scholarly Publishing.

Historians talk of the Seven Years War, the Thirty Years
War, and the Hundred Years War but rarely of the Fourteen
Hundred Years War that has been waged by the followers of
the Prophet Mahomed against those who reject their religion,
Islam. After the spectacular success of the Arab armies led by
Mahomed's father-in-law Umar after the Prophet's death, the
jihad or Holy War was waged among others by Seljuk Turks,
then Ottoman Turks, and today violently by extra-national
self-appointed bands of Islamists such as Al Quaida and
ISIS; or peaceably with petro-dollars by the Wahabi Saudis,
guardians of the Holy Shrines in Mecca where it all began.

For the first thousand years of this long war, Islam's chief
antagonists were the Byzantine and Latin Christians, led
by their emperors or, in the case of the Latins, galvanised
by popes. More recently, in the nineteenth and twentieth
centuries, the European nations triumphed and absorbed
Muslim nations into their empires but they were no longer
particularly Christian, motivated not by a militant faith but
the pursuit of their commercial and political interests. These
western interventions are nonetheless referred to by aggrieved
Muslims as 'crusades', even though the Cross has long since

been replaced by the union jack, the tricolor, and now the stars and stripes.

Moreover, as Paul Stenhouse makes clear in this final publication before his death, *Islam. Context and Complexity*, the First Crusade preached by Blessed Pope Urban II was not a precursor of European imperialism but a response to a plea for help from the Byzantine Emperor, Alexius Comnenus. 'For the Christian states bordering the Mediterranean, the period between the death of Muhammad and the First Crusade had been a 463 nightmare: a period of regular, disorganised (and occasionally well organized) bloody incursions by Muslim— mainly Arab and Berber—land and sea forces.'

Paul Stenhouse notes that his researching that schismatic group of Israelites, the Samaritans introduced him to the subject of his book. 'During the long period of my involvement with Samaritan history and traditions,' he writes in his preface, 'the intellectual and literary paths I trod were continually crisscrossed by Islam and its Qur'an, along with Islamic Law and Islamic history'.

Readers of *Annals* have long appreciated the great learning and lucid expositions of its editor, particularly on the subject of Islam about which there is considerable confusion. We are told that it is a religion of peace by Pope Francis, and the former British Prime Minister, David Cameron; yet there are regular atrocities in our cities perpetrated by Muslims inspired by verses in the Qur'an. Paul Stenhouse unravels the complexity in this series of essays which first appeared as articles in *Annals*. Some deal with the past, others with the present. He makes a distinction between religious Islam and political Islam, explaining how the astonishing success of the Arab armies under Umar was a result of both Byzantine and Persian armies' exhaustion after long wars of attrition; but also the long-running disputes between the Byzantine emperors and the peoples of their outlying provinces who 'felt no loyalty to Constantinople, and were relieved to have seen the last of the Byzantines.' The gates of Damascus were opened to the Muslim armies in 635 by, among others, the grandfather of Saint John Damascene.

Initially, the all-conquering Arab armies were more interested in power and booty than conversion; a tax, the *jizya*, enabled the 'peoples of the book', Jews and Christian—*dhimmis*—to continue to practise their religion; but pressure was put on them to *submit* (Islam means 'submission'); and although 'the majority of Christians in Arabia, Roman Syria, North Africa, Persia and Spain, remained Christians despite intolerable restrictions on their freedom for quite some years after the Arab invasion, the number of Christian bishops in North Africa declined from seven hundred in the fifth century to forty in the tenth century and by 1050 there were only five left. Christians in Islamic states such as the Caliphate of Cordova 'were not second-class citizens: *dhimmis* were non-citizens'.

The author reminds his readers that Muhammad, the founder of the supposed 'religion of peace', was capable of great cruelty, at one time ordering his enemies' 'hands and feet to be cut off, and their eyes branded with a hot iron, before abandoning them in the desert until they died'. He acknowledges that Muhammad and 'the Caliphs who succeeded him ... and the Arab tribesmen who fought their *jihads* with such reckless abandon, were children of their times

and of their desert milieu and tribal and nomadic custom';
but it is his example, and precepts found in the Qur'an, that
inspire and justify comparable atrocities today committed by
ISIS.

Those, such as this reviewer, who were fortunate enough
to have known Paul Stenhouse, will remember him as a
holy and gentle man, but these qualities do not impede him
from delivering harsh judgements on today's *jihadis* and the
moderate Muslims who are slow to condemn them. 'Can a
halt be made,' he asks, `to the preaching of hatred and the acts
of violence and inhumanity by fanatical Islamists in the name
of Allah against non-Muslims, and other Muslims regarded as
'unfaithful to Islam'? He is pessimistic. Unlike the Catholics'
pope, Islam has no accepted authority to rule that the barbaric
practices of seventh century marauders are indefensible in
modern times. He is scornful of the policy of Western nations
towards Islam, particularly the United States. He describes in
detail how the Americans deliberately drew the Soviets into
the `Afghan trap' by arming and financing the *mujahidin* who
in due course turned against them, and embroiled them in the
longest war in their history.

The author also criticises those in the west `who since
2011 have been 'cheering on the political and media pack
clamouring for Bashar al-Assad in Syria 'to go' and who
welcomed the foreign 'opposition' *mujahidin* as their numbers
grew into many tens of thousands ...' resulting in `unspeakable
violence and destruction unleashed on Syria' and `prepared
the ground for ISIS'. Above all, he laments the lack of a clear
riposte to Islamism. He concurs with the Italian senator
Marcello Pera that `the fibre of the West' is `permeated by a

mixture of timidity, prudence, convenience , reluctance and fear'. The political correctness which paralyses us may stem from a desire to atone for our nations' past misdeeds, but no good is done if it is based on the kind of historical distortions exposed in Paul Stenhouse's admirable book.

Samaritan Studies

Marek Jan Chodakiewicz

Paul Stenhouse was truly a Christian universalist in the best sense, firmly believing that we are all children of God. Thus, he made friends easily and they came in all shapes and hues. His milieu in Australia was extremely colorful in all sorts of ways. Father John F. McMahon MSC, dubbed his friend 'a priest for all seasons.' Fr Stenhouse helped immigrants, journalists, scholars, and even musicians. He was a Catholic priest of the world, without losing his bearings by descending into the morass of cosmopolitism.

He continued his education at the University of Sidney, where he earned his BA in Hebrew and Arabic languages in 1972. He also mastered Samaritan and translated Abul Fath's *History of the Samaritans*, which earned him an MA degree with honors. The translation and edition were so superb that his honors thesis metamorphized into a PhD thesis, which he based on a comparative exegesis and deciphering of almost two score of mostly damaged and corrupted Arabic manuscripts of the work.

The next logical step was to beg a leave from his work and enrol at Oxford University's St. Catherine's College for his Doctor in Philosophy degree. He never finished his degree because *en route* he was enlisted by Father General E.J. Cuskelly MSC, in Rome, to serve as his personal assistant and the chief administrator of the society's residence in Rome.

He dropped out of Oxford in 1976, but continued with his doctoral dissertation and completed it in 1980, while posted in Yugoslavia's Croatia region—namely, in Dubrovnik. Fr Stenhouse wrote his PhD thesis in three volumes based on multiple sources in multiple languages. Unfortunately, no scholar was available at his institution to assess the work. The doctoral student had to wait until a qualified dissertation reader was located.

And wait he did, but not idly. For example, during the civil war in Lebanon, Fr Stenhouse flew to Malta, where he hired a boat to smuggle medicine for the needy in the Levant. The medicine was donated by Australian pharmaceutical companies. Unauthorized and unorthodox, the mission was a success and a prime example of what the Missionaries of the Sacred Heart could accomplish. Before this audacious stunt, virtually all aid moving through the so-called proper channels had fallen into the hands of thugs and militias. Our priest figured out a way to outsmart them as well as the dead hand of international bureaucracy.

Recalled to Australia in 1981, from time to time, he gave lectures, for instance, at the College de France, where he was a member, or at the University of Tel Aviv, where he dazzled everyone with his knowledge of the Sarmatians.

Eventually, I got to know Fr Stenhouse to some degree through correspondence. He published a few articles by my wife and sister in Annals Australasia, a prime Catholic periodical. He obviously liked our stuff, and we liked his, as did others.

Catholic academic, Karl Schmude, confirms this: 'Paul Stenhouse could have lectured in any of the College's core subjects of history, literature, philosophy and theology, studied across the centuries—and, for good measure, he would have translated a Latin passage into Hebrew or Greek during the lunch break!'

I do not know much about his ministry and spirituality, aside from a sense that he was a traditional Catholic. The main point of attraction for me was his omnivorous mind, and in particular his mastery of the Middle East and east Africa. Since I have been in the process of writing a monograph on 'The Worlds of Islam' for a while now, I always cast about for sagacious insights and solid sources on the topic. Therefore, I was smitten by Fr Stenhouse's original translation of arguably the best original source on jihad, by Šîhab ad-Dîn Aḥmad bin 'Abd al-Qader bin Salem bin 'Utman vel 'Arab Faqih, his 16th century study Futûḥ al-Habaša: The Conquest of Abyssinia (Tsehai, 2003), which was further edited and footnoted by the late Richard Pankhurst, an illustrious Ethiopia expert. As my tribute to Fr Stenhouse, I would like to share some of what he made available to us in English.

'Arab Faqih's account is simply morbid. It is a rather laconic chronicle of killing and enslaving Christians, routinely massacring combatants and non-combatants alike; forcing the survivors to convert; raping their wives, mothers, and daughters; and looting, desecrating, and burning their churches. By my count the chronicle recalls that last dastardly deed in some detail perhaps 25 times (s. 32, 36, 60, 138, 144, 161, 163, 165–7, 184–5, 190–2, 222, 227, 239, 247–51, 265, 272, 304, 312, 346–7). A standard account is rather casual: 'He went … and set the church ablaze … the monks plunged into the fire, like moths dive into the wick of the lamp; all but a few of them … There was nothing wrong in burning it down' (pp. 191–2).

One sad reflection is that most captives apostatized. 'Of the patricians you captured, keep with you those who become Muslims; kill anyone who refuses' (p. 324). And then ' 'Slit the throats of all of them like slaughtered sheep … Convert to Islam … otherwise I'll do to you what I did to your leaders.' So all of them converted to Islam, great and small alike' (s. 119). Most of the conquered population stopped resisting. They accommodated the conquerors. In Gedem, for example, all 'inhabitants became Muslims' (p. 218). The same happened in Zarji, Zaquala, and other places (p. 298).

At times, Christian troops defected *en bloc* to the Muslims, sometimes giving up their commanders to escape death at their unmerciful hands. Occasionally, they'd try to re-defect, but would face slaughter if caught. 'Thereupon the Muslims pursued them, killed them, and made prisoners of them, to the very last… They were handed over to the imam who ordered them to be put to death so that the ground was covered with their dead bodies' (p. 71). Only in one instance of mass slaughter in Tegre were 10,550 Christians beheaded after a fortress fell (s. 352–3).

Examples of martyrdom are many, but most martyrs had no choice. Only a few are noted to have chosen death consciously by remaining true to their Christian faith (p. 210). At times the martyrs were Ethiopian patricians too proud to apostatize; in one instance, 500 monks were slaughtered inside their church of Abba Samuel in Sire (s. 355).

In the Muslim interpretation of the calamity, '[Imam] Ahmed [the Left-Handed] ruled the country of Abyssynia and brought it peace' (p. 20). As for the Christians, 'they are Satans' (s. 116). The author narrates the horrors matter-of-factly. He sees the mayhem as Allah-ordained and sanctified. Only sometimes do his emotions get the better of him, as when he vividly describes a holy Islamic warrior: 'And Sabr ad-Din, a fearless horseman who, if ever he saw an infidel, could not control himself until he had seized him. He was like a camel in heat. Blood flowed from his nose, so infuriated did he become for God, and so deep was his longing for the *Jihad* in the way of God' (s. 55).

The jihadis brought Christian Ethiopia to the brink of extinction. They even killed the Emperor, and most of the aristocrats. Only a joint Abyssinian–Portuguese crusade— which is not covered in the account—saved the third-oldest Christian kingdom on earth from total annihilation. The Christians united and overcame the calamity of jihad. Fr Stenhouse believed that the ancient text was relevant to the present and the future, in particular the spectre of the martyrdom of the Church.

JOHN FARRELL

Michael Wilding

In this splendid, pioneering study, *John Farrell, Poet, Journalist and Social Reformer 1851—1904*, Paul Stenhouse makes the case for John Farrell as an integral figure in the radical literary and political ferment of the 1880s and 1890s in Australia. Henry Lawson, 'Banjo' Paterson, Barbara Baynton are all remembered, but Farrell has been forgotten. He was one of the only ten writers featured amongst the 80 illustrations to A. W Jose's *History of Australasia*, first published in 1899 and in its sixth edition by 1917. Yet you will be hard put to it to find his work reprinted or discussed in any anthology or history of Australian literature today.

For the first time we have a full picture of the man. 'I as a lad worshipped him,' Henry Lawson recalled of Farrell, 'even more than I did Gordon.' Farrell encouraged Lawson's writing and loaned him money. J.F. Archibald, the founder of *The Bulletin*, recalled, 'Few men on the press of Australia at any period in our literary history have been so powerful for good as John Farrell.'

Farrell's early career was that of a brewer in Queanbeyan. One New Year's Eve a number of the lively spirits of the town called at Farrell's house and asked for drinks. 'There is nothing here,' he told them 'but I'll give you the keys of the brewery and you can go there and take what you want.' Which they did. As his fellow poet Bertram Stevens observed

'Naturally a man who ran a business on such lines was not likely to make a fortune … Farrell was quite unfitted for business management. He was far more deeply concerned in poetry and politics than in his own beer—which, by the way, he seldom drank.'

He began writing for a couple of regional papers, *The Hampden Guardian* and *The Albury Banner* from 1875 onwards. Through the 1880s he was a prolific contributor to the newly established *Bulletin*, and editor of a number of papers, amongst them the *Lithgow Enterprise* and *The Australian Standard*. And from February till October 1890 he was editor of the Sydney *Daily Telegraph*, continuing as a member of the leader-writing staff until June 1903, resigning when the paper became increasingly anti-labour in its policies.

The Bulletin was central to Farrell's writing. He wrote the first short story to appear in its pages. But it was the poems he contributed that established his reputation and popularity. 'Jenny—an Australian Story' ran for six months in 1882–3. Farrell recalled 'I wrote the opening instalment of 'Jenny' … and sent it to the *Bulletin*. I had only intended it as a specimen but Traill was in America, and in his absence Haynes shoved it in and I was bound in honour to go on supplying the copy from week to week.' With its descriptions of everyday bush life and its attendant poverty and hardships, with its sympathetic portrayal of a woman's struggles, it proved immediately popular.

At the height of the Shearers' strike William Lane published Henry Lawson's first contribution to *The Worker*, May 16, 1891, the poem 'Freedom on the Wallaby'. Two weeks later the *Bulletin* published Farrell's no less radical poem 'The

Weakness of Mr King—a Ballad of Coreena' commemorating a confrontation between strikers and strike breakers, in which the military arrested five trade unionist strikers and took them back in handcuffs to Brisbane. Henry Lawson's radical verse of the 1890s is still remembered, but Farrell's has been forgotten until now.

Farrell's verse often had a strong satiric and comic note. 'My Sundowner' is a classic tall story bush yarn. It tells of a tree at Murragumbalong which compels those who see it to hang themselves to death from its branches. The tree becomes a tourist attraction, Ned the sundowner charges people £10 a time for the privilege of hanging themselves, and having raised £30,000, goes 'home' to England, enters Parliament, and after blowing all his money on 'sprees' ends up back at Murragumbalong.

As well as a writer and editor, Farrell was a radical activist, writing and campaigning in the cause of the land nationalization and single tax movement associated with the American social theorist Henry George. The movement was given massive impetus in 1890 when George visited Australia. Farrell accompanied George at every stage of his New South Wales tour, and wrote about it for the New York *Standard*.

Henry Lawson recalled in 'Pursuing Literature in Australia' in the *Bulletin*, 21 January 1891, how as a youth 'I watched old fossickers and farmers reading *Progress and Poverty* earnestly and arguing over it Sunday afternoons.' George's *Progress and Poverty*, published in the USA in 1879, was serialized in a Sydney paper in the same year and his ideas were widely disseminated. Lawson's 'A Day on a Selection' (*Bulletin*, 28

May 1892) ends with the hilarious—or tragicomic—episode in which the selector and his neighbour attempt to discuss the political ideas of Henry George, Ignatius Donnelly and Edward Bellamy over dinner, while interruptions from children and chooks prevent anything substantial from being said, let alone done.

'Land nationalization', William Lane wrote, 'would do more in a single day than protection will do in a century towards adjusting and keeping perpetually adjusted that distribution of wealth, the present mismanagement of which is the cause of all poverty, nearly all crime, and most vice.' George's *Social Problems* was discussed by Lane in his 'Books Well Worth Reading' series in the *Worker, Progress and Poverty* was available from *The Worker* Book Fund, and George's ideas are raised in Lane's novel, *The Workingman's Paradise*. Lane and Farrell became friends, and their two families used to meet when the Lanes were living in Sydney, along with Mary Cameron (later Mary Gilmore), waiting to sail to Paraguay to establish the New Australia settlement in 1893.

Lane, like most of the radical movement, ultimately abandoned George's theories. But Farrell and others, including Catherine Spence and Rose Scott, continued to espouse them. As late as 1934 in Christina Stead's *Seven Poor Men of Sydney*, the character Baruch Mendelssohn—'my first study of my husband to be,' she said in an interview—quotes from George on how the current capitalist system crowds 'human being into noisome cellars, and squalid tenement houses, fills prison and brothels, goads men with want and consumes them with greed, robs women of the grace of perfect womanhood, takes from little children the joy and innocence of life's morning.'

The Single Tax movement was one of a number of organizations circulating radical ideas in Australia that influenced the program of the early years of the Australian Labor Party. The stress was on a single tax only—on unimproved land values—and a refusal of any tax on commodities, since commodity taxes impoverished the poor and privileged the wealthy. The conservative Disraeli had made the same point about the injustice of excise duties, which fell most heavily on the poor, in *Sybil* (1845).

Farrell's advocacy of the single tax movement was serious journalism. It also consistently alienated advertisers from the papers Farrell edited, and frequently led to their closure. But it kept Farrell in continual contact with the emergent labour and union movement.

Stenhouse records: 'Among the early single taxers who owed their start in politics to Farrell, and upon whom his influence rested long after his death were Joseph Cook, Frank Cotton, William Morris Hughes, William Arthur Holman, George S. Beeby, Walter E. Johnson, George Black, John Haynes, R. Hollis, and William Affleck.' His friendships in the political world were as equally extensive as his literary associations.

The neglect of John Farrell in the years since his death, though unjustified, regrettable and scandalous, is neither unique nor surprising. As Stenhouse succinctly remarks, 'part of the reason for this lies in his uncompromising commitment to social and economic reform.' The waning influence of the Single Tax and Land Nationalization movement further contributed to his exclusion from the literary and political record. Although Single Taxers were in the forefront of the early Labor Party in NSW, and for a while controlled the party executive, their influence waned. Of the various components of radical thought in the 1880s and 1890s, the Single Tax movement was one that was abandoned and forgotten. Forgotten to such an extent that it was a federal Labor treasurer who first proposed introducing the Goods and Services tax in 1985. What would Farrell have written about that?

Excerpted from Michael Wilding's introduction to *John Farrell, Poet, Journalist and Social Reformer 1851—1904* by Paul Stenhouse (Australian Scholarly Publishing, Melbourne).

PART III

MINISTRY

The Catholic Charity Aid To The Church In Need

Phillip Collignon

It is my privilege to put down on paper my thoughts on Fr Paul's association with the international Catholic charity Aid to the Church in Need (ACN). He gave 18 years of faithful service to the Australian office of ACN, as Chairman of the Board since its inauguration in 1997. From humble beginnings, Fr Paul provided guidance and stability, to see the Australian office of the charity now established as a reputable Catholic charity in this country, looking after the pastoral needs of the Catholic Church wherever She is poor, persecuted or threatened. We were blessed with his faithful service. During my time as National Director of ACN, Fr Paul became a great friend and mentor not only to me, but to my wife Debbie as well.

How did this connection and friendship first start? A trip down memory lane is required.

In 1947, the founder of Aid to the Church in Need, Fr

Werenfried van Straaten, a Dutch Norbertine priest, launched a campaign after WWII to help starving German refugees with food, blankets and clothing. His appeals led to a flood of generosity. When no money was available, people offered food, including bacon, which quickly earned him the nickname, the Bacon Priest. ACN supported a vast number of projects, including the training of seminarians behind the Iron Curtain, the purchase of cars and motorbikes to mobilise backpack priests, to the construction of chapel trucks—converted buses, with swing-out altars, used as mobile churches, to bring the Mass and sacraments to the scattered Catholic refugees in Germany.

Fr Christopher Coenen, a fellow Norbertine priest, coordinated the Chapel Truck mission from our HQ's in Germany back in those days and when he requested to take up the role as chaplain to the Dutch Catholic migrants in Australia in 1957, Fr Werenfried reluctantly let him go, on the proviso that he set up the Australian branch of *Iron Curtain Church Relief*, as the charity was known at that time. During his placement in Australia Fr Coenen received permission from Cardinal Gilroy the then Archbishop of Sydney to set up the work in 1965, and the Cardinal became one of our first benefactors. My father John Collignon was the president of the Catholic Dutch Migrants Association at the time and our family became very good friends with Fr Coenen. My brother and I were altar boys back then and served at many a Dutch wedding where Fr Coenen was the celebrant. To help Fr Coenen promote the work of ACN my whole family was conscripted to ready the charity's newsletter, the *Mirror*, for posting and dispatch back in those early days.

When Fr Coenen was called backed to Germany in 1968 he asked my father to continue the work of ACN. He did so until his death in 1976. My sister Ann then took over the responsibility of the work until she returned to the workforce in 1990. Up until then the work was done on a voluntary basis.

The former Secretary General of ACN, Ton Willemsen, and niece of Fr Werenfried, came out to Australia in late 1989 to find a replacement. During her visit I was appointed on a full—time basis to promote the work throughout Australia. My wife Debbie, may I add, actually began working for ACN before I did. She became Ann's part-time assistant in 1985 and continued on as my office manager until my retirement in 2018.

I started work in January 1990 and, as the work grew, HQ in Germany asked me to transition from being a Representation to establishing a board in accordance with the Statutes of our charity. I mentioned to HQ that I would need assistance with this matter and Ms Willemsen sought the advice of, at the time, Monsignor Peter Elliott, Auxiliary Bishop of Melbourne George Pell and Audrey Donnithorne, a good friend of ACN who assisted the work of the church in communist China. The names put forward for the board were Lady Mary Lawler (RIP), Johno Johnson (RIP), Terry Tobin, John McCarthy and David Scarf. My claim to fame was that I suggested Fr Paul Stenhouse as the Chairman of the Board.

I first came across Fr Paul when I was asked by HQ to invite a journalist along with me to cover the return of Cardinal Lubachisky to Lviv in Ukraine after the authorities had lifted the ban against the Ukrainian Catholics of the Byzantine Rite (UCBR) in 1989. Cardinal Lubachivsky, along with other leadership of the UCBR, officially returned to Lviv from exile on 30 March 1991. Fr Werenfried, ACN representatives and journalists from around the world were also invited to witness this historic event. Fr Paul and I were privileged to be part of this group.

So we flew to Ukraine in the first ever chartered Aeroflot flight from Rome to Lviv. I was only new to the job and I was concerned that Fr Paul was my responsibility and under my care. Needless to say, I soon found out that Fr Paul was his own man and could fend for himself quite nicely. There were times when I was in the crowds that had thronged to welcome home the Cardinal only to see that somehow Fr Paul had gained access to vantage points to get the story and the photo that great journalistic stories are made of.

On the same trip, we also travelled to Kiev to meet with Church dignitaries. Our visit just happened to coincide with the 5th anniversary of the Chernobyl disaster. The world press covering the return of the Cardinal asked the authorities to visit the site and quite miraculously, permission was granted, as little or no foreign access had been granted in previous years. Neville Kyrke Smith, the newly appointed ACN UK director had pulled me aside the morning of the visit and warned me not to go, because he feared I would be irradiated and risk not being able to father further children. Having put the fear of God into me I was in the process of quietly retreating back to my room to avoid getting on the bus, when Fr Paul came bounding down the hotel stairs full of zeal with the knowledge that we were off to Chernobyl. I tried to politely say that I thought it best that I stay in the hotel but, in his inimitable style, he managed to get me onto the bus to witness the aftermath of the disaster that occurred at the Chernobyl nuclear power plant. Needless to say it was one of the most unique experiences I have ever encountered.

Nearly fifteen years later, in 2005, Fr Paul and I were privileged to return to Ukraine to attend the opening of the Ukrainian Byzantine-rite Catholic Seminary of the Holy Spirit in Lviv Ukraine. Fr Paul had a great love for the persecuted Church and wrote numerous stories in The Annals on the plight of Christians who suffered through the ages because of their faith.

Fr Paul wrote a moving story in The Annals about his trips to Ukraine in 1991 and 2005. I feel it is important that we read in his own words what he felt as he remembered the struggles of the Ukrainian Catholics of the Byzantine Rite and how he had been inspired by the work of Aid to the Church in Need in helping this beleaguered Church rise from the ashes.

A Tale of Lazarus and a Stolen Penny

Byzantine-rite Catholics of Ukraine Reclaim Their Birthright

By Paul Stenhouse, MSC, PhD

I was standing alongside the seminary choir in the loft that overlooks the sanctuary and chapel of the Ukrainian Byzantine-rite Catholic Seminary of the Holy Spirit in Lviv in Ukraine.

With a crowd of local people and overseas visitors I was watching as His Beatitude the Ukrainian Catholic Patriarch Lubomyr Husar began the liturgy of consecration of the newly constructed, beautiful and as yet undecorated building dedicated to the Holy Spirit.

The Cardinal Patriarch, vested in blue, and with a blue crown on his head, was flanked on both sides by seventeen of his bishops from the Ukraine and from the Ukrainian diaspora — especially Canada, USA, Argentina, Brazil and Australia.

The ancient chant of the first Catholics who inhabited this region at a time [AD988] when the Duchy of Moscow did not exist, and almost a century before the Orthodox Church separated herself from the Catholic Church, filled the cupolas of the chapel.

The blue vestments were in honour of our Lady, whose

Assumption into heaven was being celebrated on this day by Eastern Rite Catholics.

I recalled one of the myriad beautiful parables preserved in our Gospel records of Jesus. Through the harmony of the old Slavonic chants I could hear the voice of our Lord as he compared the Kingdom of Heaven to a woman who had lost a penny somewhere in her house. She looked everywhere, swept the house clean, and eventually found the penny. She called her neighbours together and said to them, 'Rejoice with me, for the penny that was lost has been found'.

As I stood there immersed in the beauty of the consecration ceremony and the Mass that followed over the next three hours, I realised that the penny—in the Ukrainian version of our Lord's parable—had not been lost or mislaid but had been stolen and hidden.

When the deadly but now defunct Soviet Empire swallowed mainly Catholic Western Ukraine in 1946 the Russian Orthodox Church, by then a servile satellite of the atheistic regime also compulsorily swallowed millions of Ukrainian Byzantine-rite Catholics.

These suffered a fate similar to that of millions of their fellow Byzantine rite Catholics in Eastern and Southern Ukraine who centuries earlier had been forced to join the Russian Orthodox Church under the Tsars, and had been culturally and linguistically liquidated.

Like so many despots, however, having swallowed their prey, confiscated their Churches and Monasteries, killed countless priests, bishops and faithful, and imprisoned their Patriarch Josef Slipyi and destroyed their culture, the Communists and their allies in the Orthodox Church found the Byzantine-rite Catholics difficult to digest.

From the end of World War II in 1945 until the fall of the Communist prison-state in 1989, the once flourishing Catholics of the Byzantine-rite in Ukraine officially ceased to exist.

Their remnant survived only in the diaspora, mainly in Canada, North and South America and Australia, where bishops and priests kept the faith and traditions of this martyred Church alive.

All attempts to have their existence acknowledged proved futile. The politically correct mantra repeated endlessly by communists and Russian Orthodox alike, was that were no Catholics of Byzantine-rite in Soviet Ukraine.

In 1991 Cardinal Lubachivsky returned to Lviv in Western Ukraine from exile in Rome to take possession of his Patriarchal See, the Cathedral of St George of the Ukrainian Catholics. He was told by the Orthodox authorities not to bother coming as there were no Byzantine-rite Catholics to be found in Ukraine.

I was on the plane that bore him home. As we landed at Lviv airport we found people standing on the roofs of the airport buildings and cheering. Crowds of Catholics lined the streets as we drove to St George's Cathedral.

Over the next few days we were to be overwhelmed by the immensity of the crowd of Catholics who, religious oppression at the hands of Russian Orthodoxy and Russian communism notwithstanding, had preserved their faith, and come out of the darkness of servitude, into the light of freedom.

That triumphant Palm Sunday was unforgettable as tens of thousands crowded the square in front of the Cathedral to welcome their Patriarch home at last. I recall meeting at a formal dinner on that occasion, a former Communist bureaucrat who was raised an atheist. He lamented the fall of Communism, and told me how difficult it would be for me to imagine how he felt as his world collapsed around him. God was not supposed to exist. Where had all these religious people come from?

The past almost fifteen years flew by me as I stood alongside the choir of seminarians as they sang the responses to the long and beautifully symbolic ritual of consecration of a Church.

The liturgy of the Mass, and especially the Communion brought to the crowds who thronged the Chapel, brought tears to the eyes of many of us as we recalled the seemingly hopeless situation of the Ukrainian underground church, with its Patriarch Josef Slipyi in a Siberian prison, and the Church's very existence denied.

Along with our Australian Director Philip Collignon and many others, I was especially proud to be representing Aid to the Church in Need—the Pontifical Charity founded at the end of World War II by the Dutch Premonstratensian priest, the late Father Werenfried van Straaten.

ACN had supported the underground Ukrainian Byzantine-rite Church through its darkest days, and provided funds that educated priests and bishops and sisters as well as providing the bulk of the cost of the new seminary and providing scholarships for its two-hundred and twenty students.

Their present Patriarch—Cardinal Lubachivsky's successor, Cardinal Husar—though frail and in poor health seemed, to all of us present at the Consecration of the chapel and Mass, to vindicate the faith and sacrifice of a martyred Church; and at the same time to symbolise the hope and courage and confidence of the new generation of Ukrainian Byzantine-rite

Catholics—predominantly young, and devoted to their faith.

The pride of the more than two hundred and fifty seminarians—diocesan and religious—and of the many hundreds of faithful who crowded the chapel of the new seminary in Lviv, was palpable.

The penny that had been stolen was, at last, restored to its rightful owner. Lazarus had truly risen. And it was the Lord's doing. Alleluia. Alleluia.

The above story shows how Fr Paul became very fond of the work of Aid to the Church in Need. He loved the charity's Catholic profile and the unique emphasis it placed on assisting the persecuted and oppressed Church in whatever country she is to be found. He believed ACN offered a unique service to the Church Suffering and always argued that our charity not succumb to the temptation of becoming more oriented towards socio-charitable work, or direct evangelistic or catechetical work, or involvement in media (apart from fund-raising) otherwise it would risk seriously jeopardising its irreplaceable charism inherited from Fr Werefried. He believed other organisations were working strenuously for all these important causes. In his eyes ACN was unique in its special focus on Church infrastructure in poor and persecuted countries, and the charity's support for the Church Suffering.

In preparing for a meeting after the death of our founder, Fr Werenfried, he penned some thoughts about the dangers facing ACN. In his mind the one danger that stood out amongst others was the risk that ACN begin to act and think like other secular multinational bodies. He wrote:

We who, at least metaphorically speaking, are some-where near the apex of the ACN, can too quickly for-get our dependence on, and the gratitude we should feel and must show towards, our Catholic grass-roots base. Decisions must never be taken without consider-ing that base, and without recourse to prayer. We must never become a clone of those NGOs or government bodies that disperse charity in a soulless, indifferent, or ideologically biased way. In our case, the needy are our brethren. Those they serve are also our brethren. ACN is a Catholic family affair, and we must never lose sight of our Catholic identity.

Fr Paul also maintained that ACN had a crucial role to play in the Church of the 21st century and that, without our charity, untold thousands of people around the globe would not have access to Catholic Truth or Catholic Faith and Hope. To honour all the devoted workers who set up our work in years gone by, he believed that ACN continue with courage and fidelity to its original inspiration and never tolerate for an instant anything that might betray the special trust placed in our charity by our benefactors and the Church.

Fr Paul was a remarkable man and truly Catholic priest. As time-consuming as it was being the editor of Annals, he somehow found the time not only to represent our charity but also helped and inspired so many other people during his priestly life. He will be sorely missed but his legacy with live on through the Annals collection and his other scholarly works that reside in the walls of the Sacred Heart Monastery in Randwick.

Having known Fr Paul for over 25 years I had a wonderful opportunity to get to know him very well. We worked together, travelled together and socialised together. He was a man of great intellect who was very humble about his many extraordinary achievements. He had a wonderful sense of humour and his many interesting stories made him the centre of attention in a group.

Fr Paul suffered much in the last 10 years of his life, never complaining but still working hard on his beloved Annals and helping others, as he had always done. I will be forever grateful for the support and care that he gave to me as Director and friend. May he rest in peace.

What follows are tributes to Fr Paul from ACN colleagues in Germany and the UK.

Johannes Freiherr Heereman von Zuydtwyck,
Executive President of Aid to the Church in Need
from 2011 to 2018

There are quick friendships that don't last long and there are skeptical encounters that turn into real friendships. I experienced the latter with Father Paul.

When I first met the ACN-Presidents of the National Sections in 2011, I faced a number of very critical Presidents who disagreed with the Vatican's intervention and therefore also very suspicious of me. Father Paul was among those with a skeptical expression on their face and critical contributions. I immediately found him an interesting and impressive personality and step by step he seemed to be getting used to me. In October 2012 I visited ACN Australia. I was received very warmly and at the end of my stay I spent an entire day alone with him. These days put our relationship on a new basis, characterized by friendship and trust.

In 2013 the idea developed to set up a National Section of ACN in South Korea. The spiritual assistant from ACN International, Father Martin Barta, and I planned to fly to South Korea in September, in particular in order to win the chair of the Bishops' Conference for our plan.

Our representative asked me to strengthen our delegation with a personality that would make an impression on church leaders. And so I wrote to Father Paul: 'Your participation would certainly be a great support for the success of these discussions. You have everything that is appreciated in Korea, a respectable age, you are a priest and you are an expert on the persecution of Christians and on Aid to the Church in Need.' Father Paul agreed and with his presence and help, we were able to lay the foundations for building ACN South Korea. These days together further strengthened the friendship between Father Paul and myself and led to a trusting and fruitful cooperation. He was a priest with a great heart and mind. His death leaves a painful void, but he has a firm place in my heart.

*Regina Lynch, Head of the Projects Department of Aid
to the Church in Need in Germany*

Fr Paul Stenhouse MSC, was wisdom personified. It was not immediately obvious, as he had a talent for remaining silent in a meeting—except for the odd 'Mother Machree!'— but when he started to speak, it was clear that this was not just some ordinary smiling or bemused cleric from Down Under. He could silence a room of bankers, lawyers and experienced business men with his knowledge of the world, social communications, other religions and the Catholic Faith. I was fascinated when he spoke about Islam and his journeys and exchanges with Muslim clerics in countries that some of us might have problems finding on the map. But most importantly I will always be grateful to him for his readiness to fly half way around the world to participate in a one-day meeting of ACN in his capacity as Chairman of the Board of ACN Australia. Like all good families, there was not always unanimity on all topics at our gatherings and it was Fr Paul with his tenacity and great wisdom, who often helped us find the solution to whatever was the impasse at the time. And even when he was back home in Australia or on his travels elsewhere, he was only ever a phone call away and willing to give his advice—not only on governance questions of ACN but also on matters concerning project funding. He knew the situation of the Church in so many countries and was sure to suggest a way forward when we found ourselves facing a brick wall with providing aid to some project partners. Fr Paul is greatly missed but I have a feeling that he is continuing to smile down on us and to prod us now and then with crumbs of wisdom from that great store of his in heaven.

Project section co-worker at our HQ's in Germany

Fr Paul and his confrères were of course a precious source of information and advice on the projects we received from East Asia and the Pacific. We could draw on Fr Paul's knowledge not just for the countries but also for the way things are done in the universal Church. He was a theologian and would see aspects, qualifications, implications etc that lay people miss.

He was one of our members who had worked in Rome and knew what was appropriate and what not in the work of an institution of pontifical right. He had served the Church in many countries as diverse as Australia, the Balkans and the Middle East. His sheer years had resulted in enormous experience. All this made for a wide perspective from which he gave us wise and sober advice.

Apart from his knowledge, experience and wisdom, Fr Paul contributed to who he was. He radiated calm and self-confidence without ever being arrogant. He would think outside the box, offer unexpected perspectives and sometimes contradict apparently everyone without—at least to my knowledge—losing his gentlemanly ways. He would listen patiently and carefully. He would sit next to me while I was talking with our partners without taking things out of my hands but still—in rare cases—manage to offer his opinions when he felt the direction of the conversation could use some adjustment. And in such a serious job as ours he was, as he said, on a mission to make us laugh. He frequently succeeded.

Neville Kyrke Smith, National Director of ACN UK

It was Holy Week in Ukraine 1991 when Fr Paul Stenhouse MSC first came on the scene with Aid to the Church in Need (ACN). Phillip Collignon, the National Director of ACN Australia was looking for a journalist to accompany an ACN international group travelling to Ukraine. The group flew into Lviv on an old Soviet plane with Cardinal Lubachivsky, the Head of the Ukrainian Greek Catholic Church who had been in exile, to celebrate the resurrection of the Church after the Iron Curtain had been torn down. Suddenly, in front of tens of thousands, a figure clad in a big shiny anorak—camera in hand—had manoeuvred his way onto the balcony of the Lviv Opera House to photograph Cardinal Lubachivsky and Fr Werenrfied van Straaten, o.praem, the Dutch Norbertine Founder of ACN. There was Fr Paul! Maybe ACN was never quite the same again.

Fr Paul became the first Chairman of the board of ACN Australia in 1997. He assembled a good board and was dedicated in speaking out about the suffering of the faithful; not only did he travel to Ukraine, but also to China with an ACN group in the company of the indefatigable Audrey Donnithorne. At international meetings and in talks in London and elsewhere, his own indomitable spirit and oratory challenged, entertained and inspired audiences. Paul helped the charity to steer a course after the founder Fr Werenfried died and whilst he asked tough questions—based on his extraordinary knowledge of the Middle East in particular—he also bestowed the blessing of deep and abiding friendship on so many. He would travel the world to help a friend in need—and through Annals, often running articles and adverts on ACN—he inspired the Faith in so many.

We know that everyone will have their own memories of Fr Paul and his wonderful turns of phrase—'*Mother Machree*' included. Well—of course Paul would have known that Machree was Anglicisation of the Irish '*mo chroí*', an exclamation meaning 'my heart.' And his was a heart for the Mother of God, Mary, for Mother Church and to live by the heart. In the last edition of Annals he quoted St John Henry

Newman whose motto was *'Cor ad cor Loquitor'*. Paul's heart spoke to us through all he did with passion and fortitude; fighting the good fight of Faith with friendliness, directness, decency and good humour. He stood with the faithful who suffered and still suffer for their faith today—challenging *'slip shod Christians'* to wake up and respond, as he put it at an ACN conference in Westminster, London.

Archduke Philipp Habsburg was on the General Council of Aid to the Church in Need and he said this of Fr Paul: 'What a man and what a priest! It was so good to know him still being there with his endless knowledge, wisdom, humour and humility. We will miss him greatly.'

May he rest in peace. Amen.

'Lebanon Is More Than A Country—
It Is A Message'

Joseph Assaf

These were the words spoken by the late Saint John Paul II in the 80's and that have made their way around the world as a message of hope and unity and as a mission for Lebanon itself to be an example of, to the entire world.

'Lebanon is more than a country. It is a message of freedom and an example of pluralism for East and West,' John Paul II said. This statement went on to become a theme that he would further explore when addressing an audience of just over half a million people in Lebanon as Pope in May of 1997. His two-day visit formed part of JP II's first and only visit to the Middle East as Pope in an effort to promote reconciliation, freedom and justice in a region torn apart by war.

> 'At this exceptional assembly we wish to declare before the world the importance of Lebanon, its historical mission, accomplished down the centuries,' the Pope said, speaking in French, a second language for many Lebanese. 'A country of many religious faiths, Lebanon has shown that these different faiths can live together in peace, brotherhood and cooperation.'

The words of John Paul II must have struck the heart of my good friend Fr Paul Stenhouse like an arrow, as they often fell from his lips in the midst of many conversations I was privileged to be a part of. More than a simple nicety, Fr Paul understood the prophetic nature of St. John Paul II's observations and saw what Lebanon (and particularly its Christians) could offer, how far its influence could go and what a great mission it could have.

And he believed it.

I met Fr Paul in 1970 at the University of Sydney where he was completing his B.Arts, majoring in Samaritan Studies and Arabic. Our first encounter led to a lifetime friendship.

With the outbreak of the devastating civil war in Lebanon in 1975, it was Fr Paul who was one of the first to come to the defense of the Christians in the region—particularly the Maronite Catholics of Lebanon—who had come under the scrutiny of neighbouring countries in the region as well as a handful of countries in the West.

Fr Paul understood, that the success which Lebanon had enjoyed as a model of unity between Christians and Muslims, living side-by-side, following its independence from French mandate in 1943 was squarely thanks to the very presence of the Christians in the country.

Paul avidly argued in many instances that Lebanon's independence was in fact granted to them on the back of the political and social influence held by its majority Christian population at the time. Lebanon was a unique example of harmony in diversity—where the old and the new co-existed along with its people of 17 different religious sects and communities.

This example was the 'message' and the 'mission' that Fr Paul Stenhouse sought to promote to a world in desperate need of a model of hope, reconciliation and unity. The harmony that existed in Lebanon in the 50's, 60's and early 70's was a model that exemplified the true beauty of the commandment to 'love thy neighbour'. It was a model that Paul believed other countries in the region should espouse and he was not alone in his thinking.

The truth is that many Muslims in the region strongly believed that there was a need to preserve a Christian presence in the region. Not because they felt compelled that the Christians needed a safe haven, but rather that they saw the fruits of Christian presence across all facets of society and that they were good, true and beautiful.

Muslims of the Middle East have a saying: 'If there are no Nazarenes [Christians], it is a pity.' The saying is better in Arabic because it rhymes, but the gist is that Muslims recognize the value of having Christians in their society. Muslims aspire to send their children to Christian schools, to live in Christian neighborhoods, and to be helped by Christian organizations. Even in the midst of Christian persecution, Paul made me aware of the great mission that we as Lebanese Christians have been given to be a beacon of hope and the seed of unity within an ever-fragmented world. He made me so proud to be a witness to the idea that harmony is often born from diversity.

In 1975, at the outset of the war in Lebanon, Paul wrote a number of feature articles to a handful of publications highlighting the great contribution of Christianity to the country of Lebanon. He urged European and other Western allies especially, to step up and offer assistance in ensuring its survival in the region. He noted the historical relationship, especially between the Maronite Catholic education system and the Vatican.

Fr Paul understood the great ramifications if the world was to drive out the last Christian safe-haven in the region — especially because Lebanon was strategically positioned at the heart of the birthplace of Christianity itself.

Following a five year stint in Rome, when Fr Paul returned to Australia in the early 80's he became very involved in writing about, visiting and defending the Christians of Lebanon and its democratic political system.

I remember at the time that a cousin of mine, Msgr. John Esseff, a 3rd generation American-Lebanese priest who had never been to Lebanon until he was appointed as Head of the Pontifical Mission to Beirut in 1984 by Pope John Paul II, came to visit me in Sydney in 1986. While here, I introduced him to Fr Paul and a number of other prominent individuals that were keen to support Lebanon and the plight of Christians in the region. These included the likes of former Senator and Whitlam Minister, the Hon. John Wheeldon, former Liberal Minister and Senator, the Hon. Peter Baume and the Hon. Laurie Brereton to name a few.

These individuals had formed a committee for Lebanon in the early 80's in an attempt to achieve peace in this small but strategically important country and also because they clearly understood that Lebanon could not do it on its own in the face of foreign interference from neighbouring countries and their allies.

With a burning desire in his heart to fulfil what he saw as a divine call, Fr Paul travelled to Lebanon regularly — almost every year — including in the middle of the war to meet with many of the leaders of the country in an attempt to address the plight of the Christians of Lebanon and the greater region.

Paul knew that any war in the region would have great repercussions on Lebanon and the Christians, so much so, that even as recently as 2011, in the midst of heavy artillery and fighting with ISIS in Syria, Paul crossed the border from Lebanon to Damascus and its outskirts to meet with its leaders and offer his assistance to the marginalized.

He continued to promote the Lebanese cause fervently amongst the leaders and elite in the West as he saw it as a defining project of reconciliation and unity that would have far-reaching implications on civilization for years to come. I was privileged to have travelled with Fr Paul on a number of occasions as he actively undertook this mission and I still have fond memories of when he would stay in my family home in the village of Hardine, Lebanon. Hardine is known in history to be the first village in the mountain of Lebanon to have adopted Christianity. When St Nehmetallah Al' Hardini was beatified in 1998, Paul travelled to Rome and Lebanon with me and he covered the event in the Annals and across other media outlets.

In trying to shine a light on the important role he saw Lebanon and its Christians playing in the region, Fr Paul wrote numerous articles not only for the *Annals* but to many other mainstream publications in Australia and across the globe. His understanding of Islam and the complexities of the war in the region including the political and religious undercurrents being played out between the different religious sects was second to none. His frustrations always centred on the fact that the West failed to understand that the Christians were inevitably to be the victims of this political playmaking in an internal struggle for power within Islam.

Nonetheless, Fr Paul never gave up hope. For this, there are hundreds of thousands of Christians within Lebanon and millions scattered across every corner of the globe—especially Maronite Catholics—that are indebted to Fr Paul Stenhouse. A stalwart in the struggle for freedom and a great searcher of the truth, Fr Paul had an unshakeable conviction of the place of the Catholic Church in Christianity and indeed the world and Lebanon's role in its realization.

While he possessed the most remarkable intellect, Fr Paul's greatest asset and gift was his heart—a heart that desired nothing more than to bring humanity closer to its Creator. How fitting that this desire to defend Lebanon was so closely aligned to the very soil that Christ himself walked upon. Lebanon, in Paul's eyes was indeed more than a just a country. It was in fact, even more than just a message—for Paul, it was a mission.

An Asian Ministry

Robert Teo and members of his family

Rev Fr Paul Stenhouse's name resonates vociferously in our families, both the Teos and Liangs, and has so for nearly 40 years. My earliest recollection dates as far back as the early 80s when I came to Australia as an overseas student from Malaysia in 1983. I was converted to Christian faith at the age of 18 through the influence of a Mill Hill missionary. Mid way through my high schooling in Malaysia, I decided it was only appropriate that I set foot to seek better opportunities to support both myself and my family. I had the support of my parents and siblings to find a new place for me to settle and attempt to establish a new chapter of my life.

Migrating to a new country is always a challenge. But within that process, there are always smaller obstacles that pose doubt or uncertainty whether it would be the right decision or not. Financially, mentally and emotionally, moving away from family is always tough. However, with the right support networks and the people you meet, it makes the process of settling in all so much easier. In saying that, Fr Paul has been a very significant and influential friend and mentor that supported my upbringing here in Australia as well as for many other Asian students. His patience, dedication, and generosity of his time was admirable.

In the early years of my life as an overseas student, it was challenging to say the least, continually encountering great difficulties and always searching for assistance. It was not until December 1983 that I was introduced to Fr Paul Stenhouse at the Our Lady of Sacred Heart Church in Randwick. From thereon, Fr Paul relentlessly took the role as my problem solver, tutor, counsellor, employment agent, removalist, transporter, just to name a few. Over the years, Fr Paul had unconditionally offered his time to help the overseas students like me. His role as a religious priest extended beyond his normal 'call of duty' as a spiritual director to the faithful.

Fr Paul's regular visits to our apartment where I used to stay in Rainbow Street, Kingsford, began. The call for his help expanded exponentially as the news had spread amongst the overseas students' community. In the early years of University, I had, on many occasions accompanied Fr Paul to visit the overseas students, to check in on their welfare. A last stop at midnight would be regarded as an early shift. Fr Paul's spirit was never exhausted when it came to the 'rescue' of the students' calls and necessities.

On a lighter note, I can recall my first life experience which Fr Paul had introduced to a few of us. It was the premiere night of the Musical 'Anything Goes' at the Capitol Theatre. It was a hot summer's day, not knowingly, we were under dressed in shorts, T-shirts and 'flip-flops'. At the intermission, the men dressed in tuxedos, it was as much a cultural experience to be Australian as it was to a group of new arrivals. To this day, we still chuckle each time when the topic arises.

Regarding his language skill, Fr Paul had also picked up a few words of Asian Language such as 'Gong Xiu Ngau lau Xi' — shredded beef, 'Mat Tong Ha' — Honey King prawn just to name a few. If I may add, these are the two Asian dishes which Fr Paul loved and would order each time we went to the Chinese restaurant. To this day, I am still puzzled by the fact that despite the amount of time he had spent with the Asian Students, being a multi-linguist, I would expect his competency in Mandarin to be much better.

Over the years, the friendship developed from strength to strength. Fr Paul's network has expanded not only from his association with the students; it has also grown into a different dimension in knowing the families of the students over the years. The Liangs at Matraville — I married their only daughter.

Fr Paul became a part of our family, both the Teos and Liangs. We have had a lot of beautiful memories to honour Fr Paul who we have often regarded as a living 'Saint'. He was always a voice of reason and would be the man with all the answers. There was no problem too trivial or large for Fr Paul to solve.

In 1990, we had the honour to have Fr Paul Stenhouse to bless our marriage in the Chapel at the Kensington Monastery. He also baptised all three of our children.

Everyone in the family including acquaintances had some part of their lives touched by the amazing man we all know and loved.

Our eldest son Ben recounts:

I have always known Father Paul as a friend of the family. He was always at weekend dinners where a conversation would lead long into the night. There was always a side bowl full of his favourite ice cream and a glass of chilled white wine to accompany the discussions.

My wife and I were fortunate enough to have him

celebrate our wedding last year. Being in and out of hospital many times before the wedding, he made it his goal to be there at the mass to celebrate it with our entire family. He is dearly missed as a priest, a friend and close companion to the family.

Michael and Michelle the eldest son of Peter and Catherine Liang sum up beautifully their time spent with Fr Paul.

Father Paul Stenhouse to us meant '101 Solutions'. He was here with our family since the very day we set foot in Australia.

I migrated to Australia in 1988 and with the help of Fr Paul managed to find a job soon after. He was always there guiding me in my career and my family life, married my wife and I, and baptised both our children.

He tried wholeheartedly to make us feel more at ease in this new country where we decided to settle and build our new life. In the earlier years, he made a point of dropping by our home almost every night. We looked forward to sharing a bowl of ice cream with him after he made his rounds of visitations. While he was not overseas, he always made an effort to join us at our family dinner on weekends.

All in all, Fr.Paul was a foster father, career advisor, confidante, discussions partner, tour guide, a big and warm-hearted priest to us. He is greatly missed and loved.'

If I may add, often after dinner with the family, Michelle will have one baked butter cake ready for Fr Paul to take away to share with his fellow priests at the monastery.

Roland & Belinda and their two boys who reside in Italy had great fond memories about Fr Paul.

Fr Paul Stenhouse was more than just a priest to us; he was family. He was part of our lives since 1987—from our high school and university days, to our wedding, to the birth and baptism of our children, to house blessings from our perpetual movement of countries—Fr Paul was with us through it all. He was the 'old kwai lo' who visited every house in every country we have ever lived in.

Fr Paul was an understanding and considerate person who saw humour in life. He was a pragmatist who despite not being able to speak any Chinese (with the exception of 'wo bu shi Zhongguo ren') was keenly aware of the intricacies of a Chinese household. Over the years, we regularly shared with him our many stresses of life and were always received with a patient ear and empathetic words. Fr Paul was always there to lend a hand; time was never an issue. To us, he was the person we could always count on.

It was always a joy having Fr Paul in our home and he was an easy guest to please. One of his last adventures was to visit us in Milan for two weeks during Christmas 2017. Together, we trekked to Rome and were marvelled by his energy and good spirits despite his physical pain. He was our walking encyclopedia on the Roman ruins, early Christians, catacombs, landmarks, basilicas and popes. This trip felt like déjà vu, an experience from our 2000 Jubilee year with Fr Paul backpacking and train-hopping Italian adventure. Fr Paul loved nothing better than a plate of spinach ravioli, a glass of white wine, and a cup of tea with a generous slice of panettone.

Fr Paul did not just have an impact on us, but on our children as well. Over the years, he has proof read many theses, assignments, university applications, and even taught the children how to do proper citations. He was a great advocate of Latin and a learned scholar in Arabic, clearly evident in the wall to wall of books dating back to the middle ages which he held in his office and bedroom. As a movie enthusiast, particularly in the genre of science fiction, many fond memories and bonds were formed between Fr Paul and our children. He was the 'cool' Fr Paul because he watched all the shows they watched and knew all the characters they did. There were many laments over ice cream (vanilla, of course) on when the next season of 'Agents of S.H.I.E.L.D.' would begin.

Fr Paul was a huge part of our lives and even as I write this, I find it hard to pen in past tense as I still feel he is here with us. He will always be remembered.

Together, the Liangs and Teos continue to remember the man who helped them in all aspects of their lives. He is dearly missed, and we cannot praise him enough for who he was and who he made us become. Always bringing the Lord's light and blessing into the homes of all of those who knew him. We will cherish the memories and savour the moments spent together.

THE HOUSE OF MARY

Mary Ruth OLSH

From the back cover of the booklet, Two Novenas to Our Lady of the Sacred Heart, the Mother of God, by Paul Stenhouse MSC.

The House of Mary is a House of Prayer where each prays for all, and entrusts his or her personal intentions to Our Lady of the Sacred Heart, relying on the spiritual help of the other members of the household.

The House of Mary is the new name of The Archconfraternity of Our Lady of the Sacred Heart which has existed in Australia since the Missionaries of the Sacred Heart were established here by Father (later Archbishop) Louis-Andre Navarre in 1885.

In the intervening years, many thousands of Catholics have united their prayers with those of other members of the Archconfraternity for the good of the Church and the world.

The name The House of Mary refers to the house in Ephesus where Mary dwelt with John. It is a House where all Christians who accept Mary as their mother find a warm welcome. Non-Christians of good will are invited to find in The House of Mary their home too. Simply send your Christian first names, surname and addresses (and phone number if possible). No-one can be enrolled without his or her knowledge.

The Centre of The House of Mary (for Australia) is the Sacred Heart Monastery, Kensington: address all correspondence to

Father Paul Stenhouse MSC, Director, The House of Mary. PO Box 13, Kensington, NSW 2033.

The monthly magazine *Annals Australasia* acts as a bond between members, carries information about projected celebrations in Our Lady's honour, and helps in the living of a Catholic life through promoting devotion to Our Lady of the Sacred Heart, and publicising the missionary work of the Missionaries of the Sacred Heart and the Daughters of Our Lady of the Sacred Heart. It is available from the above address, and costs only $33 per annum (including GST) for 10 issues delivered post free to any address in Australia. Overseas rates are available on request.

Two Prayers To Our Lady

Composed by Paul Stenhouse

Prayer 1

O most dear Mother, I confide to you from this moment the whole care of my soul, trusting to you to bring it to that degree of perfection which Jesus has designed for me. I desire to forget myself in the interests of His glory. I will try this day to do all that I can for Him and for you, and in return I ask you to take care of me. Obtain for me from your divine Son the virtues He desires to see in my heart. Never leave me to my own weakness, dear Mother, but watch over me during life and come to be my safe refuge at the hour of my death. Amen.

O Virgin full of goodness, Mother of Mercy, I commend to you my body and my soul, my thoughts, my actions, my life and my death. Obtain for me the grace of loving your Son, my Saviour Jesus Christ, with a true and perfect love, and after Him, of loving you with my whole heart. Amen

Prayer 2

O my Lady, Mary most holy, God's Mother and mine. I place myself under your loving care, that you may keep special watch over me and take me into the deep embrace of your mercy. My body and soul I trust to you this day and every day and in that hour when death must claim me. In all things in which I find hope or comfort may I look only towards you, and to you may I turn in all the cares that press upon me. May I confide in you at every moment of my life, and at its close, surrender that life into your hands. Everything I have I give you, that you may always stand by me and win for me this grace, that I may perform every action of my life only as you and your Divine Son would have it done. Amen.

The Centre for celebrations for The House of Mary was in the parish church, Our Lady of the Sacred Heart, Randwick. Celebrations continue. There are boxes for placing special prayer intentions. These are collected and spoken by the parish priest to those gathered in prayer.

Josephine Ryan, longtime parishioner of Randwick remembers: The House of Mary was celebrated on the feasts Candlemas Day, Our Lady Sacred Heart, Our Lady's Birthday, Immaculate Conception. Farther Stenhouse with Asian students bought masses of flowers at the Markets. The Sanctuary and Our Lady's Altar were filled with flowers and candles. There were large spectacular banners hung either side of the Main Altar.

On Candlemas Day everyone received blessed candles. Lunch was held in the Parish Centre to which people bought a 'plate', Randwick ladies principally organised this. On an occasion of the celebrations Fr Stenhouse took over the church without first consulting the Parish Priest or Parish Staff. This didn't go over well and caused some friction. The Parish wanted to celebrate the feast of Our Lady Sacred Heart as their Parish Feast and not have it as House of Mary. Fr Peter Robinson was P.P. at this time.

People came from all areas to the House of Mary. It was

popular with the Asian communities. This is as I recall this time in the parish, I have been in the parish for forty years and have loved every minute.

We are indebted to Sister Mary Ruth OLSH for the House of Mary booklet. She continues to work for The House of Mary at Randwick.

PART IV

TRIBUTES

FROM THE *ANNALS* OFFICE

TALK GIVEN AT THE '*ANNALS* FAREWELL' LUNCH ON FRIDAY 29 NOVEMBER 2019

Peter Macinante

I welcome you all today and thank you for your generous support and contributions to *Annals* over the years.

Now I'd like to relate some memories and anecdotes from 'sources close to the *Annals* Office' or in my case, in it !

When I came to work at *Annals* in 1982, the magazine was in bad shape financially, but Fr Stenhouse was about to breathe new life into it. My co-workers were Jennie Hiatt and Andrew Mobbs.

The beautiful artwork of Hal English was to adorn the pages of *Annals* for most of the 80's. These were Halcyon days in more ways than one. Samples of the artwork of Hal and, later, Kevin Drumm appear in the final issue of the magazine.

Fr Paul's secret weapon in helping him increase the readership of *Annals* was Fr Laurie Bayliss. To supplement the wonderful articles and artwork, Fr Bayliss's secret weapon was '*Annals* CENTREFOLD'! Yes, you heard correctly. During the homily at Mass he'd hold up a closed magazine, arouse the curiosity of the congregation, tantalise their imaginations, then he'd let it drop open to reveal the centrefold … Saints for the month! Bursts of laughter would fill the church and subscriptions skyrocketed.

Between Frs Paul and Laurie, hundreds of new readers subscribed every week from parish promotions. Membership finally peaked at about 20,000.

By the way, did you know that the artist, Matthew Hatton, who created the Olly, Syd and Millie mascots for the 2000 Olympic Games, got an early boost to his career illustrating for *Annals* in 1988? Also an almost-unknown Bill Collins wrote and reviewed for Annals in the 1970s, before achieving worldwide fame as 'Mr Movies'.

The 1980s were the early days of computer publishing and Fr Paul was grateful for all the help he received. It's impossible to name everyone but way above all the rest is Greg Quinn who designed, supplied and maintained all *Annals* programmes for almost 40 years—Gratis! We can never thank you enough, Greg. Thanks also to Hendrikus Wong, Greg Tait and other friends who kept Fr Paul's PC maintained, upgraded and operational over the years.

There was no such thing as desktop publishing in the 1980's. 'Cut and paste' meant 'scissors and glue'—and that's how the editor designed and laid out the articles, which he then raced over to the courier usually to catch the last van leaving for Canberra that night. There they were typeset and returned by courier for proofreading, culminating in a drive to the printers in Canberra where Fr Paul pored over the photographic plates making any last minute corrections before each monthly issue was printed.

All this almost came to a sudden explosive end while I was driving Fr Paul back from a Canberra trip. We pulled the car to a stop at an orange traffic light unaware of a fast moving petrol tanker approaching rapidly from behind and intent on running the red light. Much terrifying screeching of brakes, skidding and jack-knifing across the busy road ensued and we escaped death by millimetres.

Many studies of Catholic faith and culture authored by Fr Paul were serialised in *Annals*. Some—such as *Why do Catholics, Catholic Answers to Bible Christians, Understanding Catholicism, Whatever happened to the Relics and Apostles and Annals Almanac of Catholic Curiosities*, have been compiled into booklets which are still available for purchase. *Annals* featured articles on all the important issues of the day from a Catholic perspective.

Fr Stenhouse re-kindled devotion to Our Lady of the Sacred Heart through the House of Mary membership, celebrations on her feast days and articles in *Annals* magazine.

Fr Perpetual Motion he was to us—always racing off to important commitments here and overseas. He never refused to help a worthy cause. Unlike the mother of the Maccabees he just couldn't say 'No'. 'Andiamo' was his war cry. 'Mamma mia, this isn't getting the baby bathed', and off he'd race to another wedding, baptism, funeral or meeting. He seemed to need everything 'immediately if not sooner'. We taunted him about this. 'Mother Machree'! he'd reply.

He sought to set the record straight on Islam. His last series of articles he compiled into a book, *Islam—Context and*

Complexity. He supported the work of 'Aid to the Church in Need' in *Annals* and was its Australian chairman for many years, as well as being on the Board of several other Catholic organisations.

He reported from war torn parts of the world the plight of persecuted Catholics. Lebanon, the Balkans, eastern European and central Asian countries and others were the subject of many articles from our 'on site' reporter. We never saw an itinerary for his overseas trips—covert operations (for his own safety we assumed), like his visit to Timbuktu.

This is where I now have to confess that (out of curiosity) Jennie and I carried out our own covert operation on Fr Paul himself. Someone had given him an enormous wave ski which he would strap to the roof racks of his car and disappear—allegedly to paddle from Watsons Bay, down Sydney harbour to the Opera House and back. We just had to check this out, so we gave him a head start on one of these occasions, followed and took up position behind a tree at the tip of Darling Point. Lo and behold he came paddling energetically past us heading in the direction of the Opera House.

Back to the office! How could we have doubted him? That was the end of our covert operations.

Just to highlight how scrupulous he was about accuracy, he'd search out original sources he wished to quote no matter how long it took, or just not use them. He claimed only to be a fluent speaker of about five languages but could read and write in at least another five or more. He just could not abide the butchering of the English language in its daily usage and was quick to point it out.

Father Paul lives on in our treasured memories of him. *Annals* and his legacy live on in the fruits of all his works, books and numerous articles. He put all his final energies into producing the last issue of *Annals Australasia* (No.9/10,2019). Copies are still available on request. He intimated to me that he may not have been able to complete it without the constant nursing care given him by Therese Compton over his final month or more. Therese, your wonderful loving example to us all must not go unacknowledged. Thank you so much with all our hearts.

Special thanks also to Peter Beswick for his most generous help over the years and to all *Annals* benefactors. And thanks to all members of the monastery community over the years for their support.

A few final anecdotes. In the Hospice I asked Father to intercede for my family with Our Lord when he reached Heaven, to which he humbly replied that he thought his first role in the afterlife would be penitential.

Earlier he had told me that according to the doctors his only sound organ was his heart. I told him 'Father, you're ALL heart'. Amidst all his pain, that really made him smile.

Just to emphasise what a tight budget *Annals* survived on over the years, Father's favourite response to financial constrictions was 'Hang the expense, give the canary another seed!' And remember, you can all treasure the memory of *Annals* and Father Paul Stenhouse by buying the publications he lovingly produced during his many years at the helm of *Annals*.

Ciao, Fr Stenhouse
Ciao, *Annals*
Ciao, good friends

A Tribute

Hendrikus Wong

Fr Paul Stenhouse was an Australian legend, a priest, missionary, scholar, and photographer. He was a talented priest with many abilities and skills ranging from languages to theology and who like to travel around the world

How we met

Our family is from Indonesia and we are of Chinese background. we migrated to Australia in 1987. I met Fr Paul Stenhouse in 1992, when I came from Indonesia to Sydney to enrol as a university student. Before meeting Fr Paul Stenhouse I was already in contact with the MSC. When I was at school, it was the nuns of the OLSH who helped me to convert to Catholicism. After my conversion, I continued to keep in close contact with the MSC and DOLSH, which led me to meet Fr Paul Stenhouse when I came to Sydney for university.

When I came to Sydney, Fr Paul was working on a book together with Henryk Skrzynski, a survivor of Auschwitz, titled *The Jewess Mary*. He typed up his book on a Macintosh computer and was having trouble converting it into a format that would allow him to open it on a Windows computer. Fr Paul was looking for someone to help him solve his problem. Someone referred him to me and that was how I met him. I helped Fr Paul to convert his file, but that was not the end of our relations, but rather, the start of a long and deep friendship. I ended up doing the type setting for the whole book. It took me a while to do this because the laser printer was not common in that day so I had to rely on the dot-metric printer, which printed pages at a much slower rate. After a few painstaking months of correction we finalised the book and published it.

After I finished my postgraduate studies, I went back to Indonesia. I found work there, got married and had two kids. I was not planning to come back to Australia, but in May 1998 there were anti-Chinese riots. These riots were violent and dangerous. I had not considered moving my family to Australia but because their safety was in jeopardy, my wife and I decided to move in the space of a day. We arrived in Australia with our two kids and a few clothes. After arriving in Sydney, I contacted Fr Stenhouse and he offered me a casework job with Chevalier Press. I worked with two other people, who after some time left, leaving me to look after the whole operation by myself. During that time, I spent a lot of time alone with Fr Paul and it was through this I got to know him very well. When working with him, it was a routine for me to drive down into town with him to have lunch. We were often accompanied by some of his friends.

Working with him

Through working with Fr Paul and developing a deep friendship I saw clearly that he was a holy priest. He was a social conservative and a highly talented scholar, specialising in Islamic studies. Fr Paul was a defender of the Church and the Catholic tradition. Fr Stenhouse was a great friend and supporter of Cardinal Pell. He continuously defended him, always pointing out the errors of the Victoria judicial system and the bias of the ABC. Over his life, Fr Paul wrote extensive amounts of articles and books, with his last one being published last year, a few months before his death, titled *Islam: Context and Complexity*.

Fr Paul was very much involved in academic institutions. He was on the board of Catholic Weekly, St John's College and was also involved in the University of Notre Dame and Campion College. He would at times visit university campuses to give lectures. It must be noted that Fr Paul was not only a talented man, he was also a very hard worker. Fr Paul always liked things done well. He was always busy with phone calls and meeting but despite this, he seemed to always have a lot of energy. He always had something to do. After finishing an edition of the *Annals* his mind would always quickly towards the next one.

Two things that Fr Paul Stenhouse loved were travel and photography. When travelling, Fr Paul would always pack lightly, taking only his work papers, clothes and most importantly his camera in his black duffel bag. He used to take a lot of photos on his travels, some which you can see today on the cover of the *Annals*. He preferred to use his own photos than to pay to use someone else's.

When he was young, we used to call him 'the Indiana Jones' priest because he loved travelling. He got this name because he would go travelling to Europe two or three times a year and would often go around in an army jacket. However, as he grew older, he donned the usual priestly attire—black pants and a white shirt. Fr Paul was also renowned for his driving skills. For this we called him 'the formula uno' driver.

Although Fr Paul was a busy and hard-working man, he was also a man who knew how to give his time to others and above all to the Church. Fr Paul was a holy priest totally dedicated to the Church. Fr Paul was a cheerful and generous man. One thing I remember about him is that he liked to say words like 'Mamma mia' and 'ciao'. Since Fr Paul was such a cheerful and generous man, he found it very easy to make friends. He was always making friends. Over time I met many of his friends, who he had no hesitation to introduce to me.

Fr Paul had plenty of friends from many different backgrounds. Fr Paul had friends both who were rich and poor. He even made friends with some politicians. Fr Paul devoted much time to his friends and helped each one of them to deepen their relationship with God. Fr Paul helped people to get close to God in other ways. He would spend a lot of time on running catechism classes for people preparing to be baptised. He would hold these classes even though there were only one or two people. Fr Paul would also frequently spend time hearing the confessions of those who came to the monastery. On occasions he would give classes for couple preparing for marriage. One thing that was notable about Fr Paul was that he had a great devotion to Our Lady. Every year he would celebrate a Mass dedicated especially for Our Lady at the Our Lady of the Sacred Heart Church in Randwick.

I like to finish by saying three things about Fr Paul.

Firstly, I would like to stress that Fr Paul was a very generous man and that I am truly in debt to him. With the support and the recommendation of Fr Stenhouse our family was selected to attend The World Meeting of Families in Milan in 2012. On this trip our family made unforgettable memories. This would have been impossible without the support of Fr Stenhouse. Our family is in debt to him for his kindness and generosity.

Secondly, that he was a good shepherd. My friendship with him was also a path that led me to become close to Christ. Fr Paul spent a lot of time explaining Church doctrine to me. Through his direction I have been able to follow Christ more closely.

The third thing I would like to say about Fr Paul is that he was a good sheep. Fr Paul followed Christ faithfully for his whole life. For the span of his life celebrated the Mass well and prayed with faith and fervour. This sustained him and through this he was able to stay on the path, following Christ closely from behind. He followed Him through the highways of Europe and the byways of Australia. He kept on following Christ closely, never stopping to rest or lag behind, and now he has followed Him through the gates of Heaven, where he will now remain for the whole of eternity together with Our Lord.

Ciao Fr Paul

ANNALS COMPUTER SYSTEM

Greg Quinn

I first met Fr Paul at the end of 1984. He had purchased a new computer from a business colleague of mine, the purpose of which was to record all the subscribers to the Catholic magazine *Annals*, to facilitate the mailing of the magazine by printing labels showing the names and addresses of the subscribers, to produce accounts and to record the payments received. At the time I was employed as a computer programmer so had the knowledge to develop a suite of programs for him.

Fr Paul maintained that he knew nothing about computing or data processing; however, when I asked him about how he wanted to use the computer, I found that he had a very clear plan and well written documentation which told me in great detail exactly how he wanted it all to work.

I understood that *Annals* could not afford to pay much for computer software so I offered to do the job for him in my spare time. Every Saturday I visited the monastery to work on his computer system. Because of his well written specifications, this work was considerably easier than it otherwise might have been.

On these occasions, Father regularly invited me to have lunch or dinner (or both) with him at the monastery, which gave me the opportunity of meeting a number of the priests and brothers who were residents there. Sometimes we would go to local restaurants instead. However, I soon discovered that he was not interested in fancy restaurant meals but preferred hamburgers, so we became regulars at the local McDonalds. Years later, he confided to me that he preferred Hungry Jack's burgers, so from then on we would go to the nearest Hungry Jack's. It was during these moments of relaxation that we developed a close friendship which continued until his passing in November 2019.

I really admired Fr Paul's work ethic. During the whole of the thirty-five years that I knew him, he worked seven days a week on *Annals* and other important projects. Even when he was in hospital for long periods in 2012, he still worked on the magazine. On Sundays, he had a hectic schedule, visiting parishes all over Sydney to say Mass. He also took these opportunities to promote *Annals*, giving away many free copies on each occasion.

Father Paul's work was not just academic, but practical as well. In his life, he must have helped hundreds of overseas students attending the University of NSW and other tertiary institutions to find accommodation and settle in. He was always willing to listen to my problems and suggest practical solutions which, upon reflection, indicated a great deal of wisdom in the affairs of everyday life.

When it came to helping people, Fr Paul was not averse to physically demanding work. When I shifted house in 1986, Fr Paul was there, sleeves rolled up, and together with his cousin Peter Macinante, helped me to load up all my furniture and other belongings, transport it to the new house, and unload it.

He was also very generous. Earlier in that same year, when my brother Peter and his wife and family came from New Zealand to visit me, my car was too small to accommodate them all, so I would have been unable to pick them up from the airport, show them around Sydney, and take them back to the airport at the end of their stay. I casually mentioned this to Father, and he immediately told me that I would be free to use his car for the whole of their stay, which was about one week.

When I married in 1988 Father helped me with all the arrangements and officiated at the wedding. Later, when I purchased a home, he came over and blessed the house for me. Over the years, he helped me in many other ways as well, too numerous to mention here.

I emigrated from New Zealand in 1978, but did not take up Australian citizenship after the normal five-year waiting period. When Father became aware of this, he urged me to do so. I realized that he was right, and that becoming an Australian citizen was long overdue. My application was accepted and in 2003 Father attended my Citizenship ceremony at the Opera House in Sydney.

When Father became ill, 1 visited him frequently and sometimes took him out to meals. I visited him a few days before he moved to the Sacred Heart Hospice, and was shocked by how much his health had deteriorated since I had last seen him, which had been only three weeks earlier. He still wanted to share a meal with me, so I helped him to my car and we drove down to Hungry Jack's for the last time. We each had a bacon deluxe, after which we drove over to La Perouse. The sun was just setting and I parked the car in a spot overlooking Botany Bay. The view was beautiful and I was glad to have been with Father on that last occasion.

Father Stenhouse was a very special person. He was hard-working and devoted to his duties, he was highly academic but willing to help out with physical work when necessary; he was wise, compassionate and generous, and was always available to lend an ear and provide sound advice. For a whole thirty-five years he was one of my best friends, and his passing has left a huge gap in my life, as I am sure it has for so many other people whose lives he touched.

Requiescat in pace

FROM *ANNALS* CONTRIBUTORS
THE STENHOUSE IRREGULARS

James Murray

The title is owed to one of the most distinguished of *The Stenhouse Irregulars*, Dick Hughes; in addition to his normal work, he was doing subbing stints for *Annals Australia* as it then was.

That's the Dick Hughes who left behind the question: was he a more skilful sub-editor than he was a jazz-pianist whose international venues included the Shakey—the Shakespeare—Surry Hills, Sydney, up the road from News Limited.

Dick Hughes, son of the legendary Foreign Correspondent Richard Hughes who inspired the Ian Fleming character Dikko Henderson in *You Only Live Twice*.

Dick was also a Sherlock Holmes scholar and a member of the Baker Street Irregulars, hence The Stenhouse Irregulars, headquartered, not at 221B Baker Street, London, but at the Monastery of the Sacred Heart, No, 1 Roma Avenue, Kensington NSW (mail: P.O. Box 13).

For me, the key to recruitment was the Anglo-Franco-Corsican—Australian Paul Fregosi who joined The Free French Navy as a teenage matelot and rose to the rank of Commander.

His duty included nine months at Cockatoo Island (metric measure corvette in an imperial measure dockyard).

He fell in love with Australia and at war's end returned here with his wife, planning to be a farmer. Reading up on the subject in the Mitchell Library, he met a journalist researching a history piece for *The Daily Telegraph*.

Told the fee, Fregosi switched his talents from farming to hacking.

When we met (introduced by Edwin 'Ted' Shropshire Morrisby, of whom more later) Fregosi had published Dreams of Empire (about Napoleon's planned campaigns not least the conquest of Australia) praised by Graham Greene and Conrad Black.

Fregosi was working on his second book, *Jihad in the West* (prophetic of 9/11/2001) and asked me if I knew anyone who was writing on the subject.

My reply: I had read some 'good copy' in *The Australian*, by-lined Paul Stenhouse and understood he was based at a monastery in Kensington.

En avant! was Fregosi's motto as an Agence France Presse journalist. He went to the monastery and, in the mediaeval tradition of travelling scholars, met Father Paul Stenhouse, fluent in French, and taken with the projected Fregosi work.

Synchronicity! Ted Morrisby had begun to organize lunches at The Journalists Club, now gone from its Surry Hill's location leaving a mystery: how could such a club (24/7 year-round licence have to be sold for property development?)

But that's by the way: Fregosi invited Father Paul along. The rest, as we used to say, is history or more exactly a list of The Stenhouse Irregulars, not in alphabetical order, but more or less as they occur to me by way of contrast.

The issue of *Annals* containing my *Media Matters* column

confirmed my notion; it displayed the by-line Rupert Lockwood. The one and only, he had a part in the Royal Commission into Espionage (1954–5). Not a bit part: he faced an allegation of being a Soviet spy, and in1969 left the Communist Party after the Soviet invasion of Czechoslovakia.

His books included *Black Armada* and *War on the Waterfront. Yet* before he died in 1997 his final single-page columns were in *Annals,* replete with good sense and hints of serious contacts.

By contrast Cliff Baxter's columns were those of a perdurable traditionalist: incisive, succinct, befitting an ABC journalist and the secretary of the Latin Mass Society.

Ted Morrisby was anything but succinct. He had, however, a lot not to be succinct about: ex-Sydney University (rusticated), ex-AAP Lion Court off Fleet Street, where his tasks included scissoring Fleet Street newspapers, putting the cutting in airmail envelopes and posting them to clients for printing under the byline, From Our Own Correspondent.

As advance man for the BBC's Alan Whicker, Ted Morrisby had been everywhere. As evidence, he would exhibit a scar he claimed was the result of an Andaman Islander shooting with a bow-and-arrow at the helicopter he was aboard.

He was also ex-News Chronicle, ex-Manchester Guardian, and Ex-ITN Africa-hand at a time when you lived off your exes and banked your salary.

Through Grundy Television, he introduced drama documentaries to Australia with *The Wreck of the Batavia* and *The Portuguese Discoverers of Australia.* On the latter we worked together as we did on *Gold, Silver and Bronze: Australians at the Olympics,* based on Gary Lester's definitive history.

Besides Fregosi, the Morrisby circle (or circus) included

Murray Sayle, Phillip Knightley, Rex Lopez and the great and generous actor Stanley Meadows.

(Around this time, I should add, Father Paul asked me to take over movie reviewing, a daunting task since I was succeeding Father Peter Malone, who remains the cineaste's cineaste world-wide.)

In fact Anthony G. Evans—alias Tony or 'Good Evans'—was better qualified but based in Perth he was off the main preview circuit

Of The Stenhouse Irregulars, he was the most formal. He had his wild side, however, the wildest working with the British film maker Ken Russell, maestro of outrage, on *Amelia and the Angel* which turned out to be part of Russell's reversion to his ancestral Catholic faith.

In conversation and print Tony Evans made less of this film experience than he could, as he did of his ABC TV experience in Perth, WA.

His *Annals* pieces, particularly on the BBC post-modern adaptation of G.K. Chesterton's Father Brown stories, had all the wisdom he brought to his books, above all his classic biography of William Wardell, revert to Catholicism, and architect of St Mary's Cathedral, Sydney, and St. Patrick's, Melbourne.

Typically of Father Paul he introduced Tony and his wife Claire (née Kelly) to me and my wife Jenny (née Pritchard) at a working lunch over the 'best pizza in Australia'—aptly with a tincture of vino at The Australia Hotel in the Rocks, Sydney.

Born 1931 like Rupert Murdoch and me (Depression Boomers!) Tony died in 2018, aged 90, back home in England with his wife and daughters at his bedside.

Only one of Evan Whitton's distinctions, Quintuple Walkley Award winner, is necessary to mark his high calibre. His last printed copy by my estimate (and I subbed it) appeared in *Annals Australasia* (issue March, 2015) three years before his death aged 90.

Headlined (by Whitton) THE LAW'S FIRST XI—FOR GOOD OR ILL his copy said (among some 900 words): 'Pope Innocent III devised a truth-seeking (Inquisitorial) legal system in the 13th century. In the 21st century Pope Francis has called for a moral face to human activity.'

As editor Father Paul chose the break-out quote which gives the bootleg flavour of the piece: 'Lord Herschell (1837–99, Chancellor 1886/92–95) He was one of 12 corrupt Chancellors who kept a will case going for 117 years while lawyers emptied a huge estate. In 1894, he invented a rule which conceals evidence of a pattern of criminal behaviour. For 120 years, his rule has enabled countless repeat offenders—serial rapists, organized criminals and their ilk—to escape justice.'

And that makes Whitton one of The Stenhouse Irregulars. It must also be said that his *Annals* pieces did not go without rebuttal by lawyer readers, an unsurprising reaction.

His bibliography runs from *Can of Worms: A Citizens Reference Book to Crime and the Administration of Justice* through *Trial by Voodoo: Why the Law Defeats Justice & Democracy* to *Serial Liars: How Lawyers Get the Money and Get the Criminals Off*.

In military terms, Michael Wilding's becoming a Stenhouse Irregular was rather like a commando joining the Peace Corps. To go through his CV would overbalance this essay.

Suffice it to say that his main distinction is Emeritus

Professor of English Literature, University of Sydney, and the country's most prolific panjandrumof letters. He wrote a foreword and got it published at Australian Scholarly Publishing by Nick Walker who also published Father Paul's last work, *Islam: Context and Complexity.*

Wilding's aid to Father Paul was crucial in completing the final issue of *Annals Australasia.*

This contained Wilding's double-page blast at the parlous state of university education, a topic on which he was pre-eminently qualified to comment given his university experience here, the UK and the US (from which he imported Creative Writing courses).

His academic career encompassed the three systems of university education: Commonwealth Scholarships. Whitlam Free and Student Loan. No prizes for guessing which system Wilding thought drew superior candidates.

To his other *Annals* contributions, over an all, too-short period, Wilding brought the elegance of Isis, the Oxford magazine of which he was editor in a distinguished line that includes Hilaire Belloc.

Sometimes mistaken for the actor-dancer who married Elizabeth Taylor, Wilding was a soloist of the counter-culture; his time at the University of Oxford, it seems to me, has given him respect for the eternal counter-culture on which his university, including All Souls, was founded as were so many of the world's.

Christopher Dawson, ex-Harrow and Cambridge, ex-*Yorkshire Post*, ex-*Daily Express*, ex-*Sydney Morning Herald*, ex-*The Australian*, ex-Cameron Highlanders (TA) was The

Stenhouse Irregular who brought to his contributions the brevity he practised as a leader-writer and military historian.

I will now flatter him by imitation—with the addition that he is the only person I have met whose family tree records the fact his ancestors paid the fines for Mass-going.

Which makes me think that if the Stenhouse Irregulars had one trait in common it was that they were pilgrims who found a compass in *Annals Australasia*.

Neither last, nor least Giles Auty, the former art critic of *The Spectator* who did not remain at *The Australian* because his views differed from that of local practitioners.

Perhaps this may have been because Auty was a fine wine that didn't travel like the one described by Hilaire Belloc in *The Path to Rome*.

But Auty, working from his base in the Blue Mountains, did travel well in *Annals Australasia*: discursive, erudite, witty. Nor was he the only wine that didn't travel well: Sir Larry Lamb, a legendary editor of *The Sun* came to the editorship of *The Australian* with high hopes and left in low dudgeon to play a part in a Robert Holmes a Court $1.8 billion misadventure: trying to take over Rupert Murdoch's fiefdom.

Although he insists he was only a Minor Counties player Auty brought to his writing the dash of CB Fry, the Test cricketer the Albanians wanted to be their king.

There are now so many ex-*The Australian* staffers that the thought occurs that if Holmes a Court had succeeded, Rupert Murdoch (Papal Knight) could have been a recruit, fit for The Stenhouse Irregulars.

Too much? Not at all: Peter Coleman, State and Federal politician ex-editor of *The Bulletin* and *Quadrant*, was a recruit as chairman of *The Annals Australasia* board, his last earthly appointment.

And who else as The Stenhouse Irregulars liaison officer than *Annals Australasia* administrator Peter Macinante?

In 25 years of working with Father Paul Stenhouse—and he was the kind of editor who made you think you were working with him not for him—what came through were his gifts as a journalist, formed during a boyhood stint on his local paper *The Camden News*.

This makes him the only editor, met during a 50-year-plus stint in the verbiage fields, who went from hand-setting type to digitally-formatting a magazine.

He wore his learning lightly, though it was not light, as his MA, PhD, and his expertise in Samaritan scriptures and Islamic studies indicated.

Punning right along with Bing Crosby and Bob Hope I'm Morocco-bound to say I think the closure of *Annals Australasia* was premature, in the light of the loyalty of its readers who not only bought it, but donated to it, pioneering a practice imitated by *Guardian Australia* on line.

Nonetheless, historians of Australasia will surely add the *Annals* bound volumes comprising 130 years of history to those of *The Bulletin* to get a bi-optic view of old controversies and the ever-new gospel of salvation.

None of this detracts from Father Stenhouse's priestly activities which had a special focus on the Lebanese and Chinese communities as well as his informal chaplaincy to local journalists.

He regaled me with an anecdote about his travels on the ground in the Middle East where he wrote a cheque or two to cover living expenses.

Those cheques were not cleared; they float among all the other currencies of the region. I like to think this is symbolic of Father Paul Stenhouse and the credo he spread as a member of the Missionaries of the Sacred Heart.

Remembering him, I think of a boyhood anthem reserved for bishops: *Ecce Sacerdos magnus*—behold a great priest!

To which may be added, *Et lux perpetua luceat ei*—And let perpetual light shine upon him, as hopefully he assists the Recording Angel with improving the CVs of his Irregulars and other scribes.

HOPE IS NOT LOST

James Franklin

After one of my wide-ranging discussions with Fr Paul, I remarked that the alphabeticity of Ugaritic and the survival of the Lollards are topics on which we hear all too little these days. The vast breadth of his understanding of virtually all subjects in the humanities made him a joy to talk to, provided one could keep up. At our last meeting, a few months before he died, he reminisced about his considerable personal relationships with both Géza Vermes and Rupert Lockwood. I admit I was rather proud of myself to be able to show I knew who both of them were. (For the benefit of the young people of today who may be reading this, Vermes was one of the most celebrated and controversial scholars of the New Testament; Lockwood was possibly the best-known Australian Communist of the 1950s as the author of the notorious Document J that played a central role in the Petrov Royal Commission, later a Catholic and contributor to *Annals*). Again, Fr Paul's breadth of understanding and ability to deal in a cooperative and civilised way with a huge range of people was evident.

I first saw Fr Paul in action in the 1980s when he gave a lunchtime talk at the University of New South Wales, where I was a young academic. The topic was the threat to the Christian community in Lebanon posed by the war then in progress, which he said threatened to turn into a genocide.

Though I did not get to know Fr Paul at that time, I saw that he was someone highly intelligent and well-informed who was telling truths at odds with the received ideas that constituted the 'progressive' narrative common to Australian universities and other cultural institutions.

Since 1999 I appreciated Fr Paul's encouragement to publish in *Annals* articles on diverse topics such as Australian freemasonry, myths about the Middle Ages, the Grameen bank, the missions to aboriginal Australians of Bishop Gsell and other Missionaries of the Sacred Heart, and Catholic philosophy. What other editor would cope with, or even understand, such diversity?

I am glad to have been able to do some small things in return. The problem with *Annals* was that it was not an online magazine, so its past issues were hard to access. Around 2013 F. John Loughnan created a huge and well-indexed archive of past *Annals* archives, but unfortunately it later disappeared from the Web. I recalled that in the online world, 'the truth is out there' (usually). I found Loughnan's site in the web archive, wrote a short Wikipedia article on *Annals Australasia*, and linked to the archive. So most of *Annals'* past—except the last few years—can be seen by going to the link at the bottom of the Wikipedia article. Just search for 'Stenhouse' to be flooded with gems ...

I am pleased too that he reacted with more than usual pleasure to my last contribution to *Annals* (Jan/Feb, 2019), reviewing a book by his friend the American Catholic philosopher Jude Dougherty. Fr Paul was undoubtedly saddened that in recent times the tide of intellectual life in western countries seemed to be flowing in the opposite direction to the one he championed based on timeless truths and reason. While he maintained optimism for the long term, the threat of closure of *Annals* and the disconnection of most of the younger generation from classical ideas concerned him. I concluded my review, addressing him personally as much as readers in general:

Hope is not lost, because the resources of civilization are still available. Each new generation faces its own choice of what among the smorgasbord of traditions to accept and what to abandon. The Internet, for all its tendencies to vacuity and pointlessness, does make available and easily accessible a range of intellectual resources unimaginable in the past. Young brains are not as damaged by malnutrition, blows to the head, measles and arsenic in the wallpaper as were earlier generations. A proportion of young intellects will grasp the truth.

If hope is not lost, it is because intellectual leaders like Fr Paul understood what had to be preserved and renewed to get us through threatening times. Few have performed that task with such knowledge, humanity, humour and charitable dealing with people as Fr Paul. And of course, with such perfection of typographical detail.

'Dipped In Ink'

Michael Wilding

It was James Murray who was instrumental in my meeting Father Stenhouse. I had recommended a couple of James' novels for publication to Nick Walker's Arcadia Press, and James had reviewed my *Wild Bleak Bohemia* about Marcus Clarke, Adam Lindsay Gordon and Henry Kendall for *Annals Australasia*, for which he was media and movie columnist. James turned up one day with a heavy, bound volume, a thesis from the University of New England which Father Stenhouse the editor of *Annals* had written some years earlier. Its topic was the journalist, editor and poet John Farrell. I knew of Farrell as a friend of Henry Lawson and William Lane, and as an advocate of the Single Tax movement, one of the radical organizations for achieving social justice in the late nineteenth century. But apart from that I knew nothing of Farrell. His satirical, political poetry from *The Bulletin* was forgotten, and none of the critical and scholarly studies of the writing of the period dealt with him. I read the thesis with increasing excitement. Here was an important, scholarly account of a major figure. Here was a major contribution to the literary and political history of the 1890s. I turned to the title page again and yes, it had been submitted for a Master of Arts degree. I was astounded that it was not a doctoral thesis.

When I met Father Stenhouse I mentioned my surprise that it had not been submitted for a doctorate. He already had a doctorate from the University of Sydney for a thesis in Samaritan studies, he replied. He had modestly felt that two doctorates might seem excessive. Samaritan studies was his area of scholarship and research, the area in which he had published, a world away from nineteenth century Australian literature. The Farrell project, it emerged, had been written out of a sense of family responsibility, if not quite obligation. Farrell was his great-grandfather. Comprehensively and indeed massively researched, discovering and identifying some 130 poems Farrell had contributed to *The Bulletin* and other journals, covering Farrell's editorship of a succession of regional and single tax newspapers and—for a brief period— the Sydney *Daily Telegraph*, the thesis had been written almost as a diversion from Father Stenhouse's multitude of duties and scholarly activities.

I don't think that Father Stenhouse had ever thought to publish the thesis. It had been written back in the 1980s, but almost nothing had been written about Farrell in the interim. I recommended it to Nick Walker for Australian Scholarly Publishing and he readily accepted it. Preparing it for publication involved getting the original typescript scanned and digitized and the updating of some of the references to Farrell's associates on whom more recent studies had appeared. It all took time and labour but, amidst all his other activities, Father Stenhouse finalized the text and the book duly appeared in 2018.

We used to meet every month or so during this period and afterwards, checking though footnotes, standardizing references, and then we would have a light lunch at one of the shopping malls near the monastery. And this was how I was drawn into writing regularly for *Annals*, which he had been editing since 1966, apart from four years in Rome in 1977–81. For like John Farrell, Father Stenhouse and I had that fascination with print media, with writing for and editing papers and magazines and setting up publishing houses. I had developed the bug at school and continued at university and began reviewing for *The Bulletin* soon after I came to Australia in my early twenties. Father Stenhouse had left school at twelve and been trained as a printer on a local newspaper. 'He has spent all his priestly life as a journalist' the author's note to his translation of *The Conquest of Abyssinia* announced. The first piece I wrote for *Annals* was about magazines, and how their hey-day seemed to be over, radio, television and the internet superseding them. The last piece I wrote was for the last issue that Father Stenhouse edited, surveying the handful of publications in Australia that had survived as long as *Annals'* 130 years. *Annals* was like a refuge for me, as one by one magazines and newspapers shrunk in size or ceased publication altogether.

Father Stenhouse's interests and concerns had an extraordinary range. Journalism was only a part of them. He translated Samaritan texts and wrote monographs on Middle Arabic grammar. His scholarly work on Samaritan studies had expanded into an interest in both historical and contemporary issues in the Middle East, and he wrote on these topics for the *Australian*, *Catholic Weekly* and *Sydney Morning Herald*. Most recently he wrote a series of studies of the history and contemporary practice of Islam, which he published in *Annals* and then collected in book form. He was planning to publish it through Chevalier Press, which he had established in 1971. I suggested he contact Australian Scholarly Publishing, who had published *John Farrell*, about finding a reliable and inexpensive printer, and Nick Walker promptly and enthusiastically responded that he would like to publish the book himself in his Pamphleteer series. And so *Islam: Context and Complexity* duly appeared in 2019.

I valued these regular meetings with Father Stenhouse. From him I learned something of the history and complexity of Islam and of Middle Eastern politics. Our conversations ranged from the medieval to the modern, from the literary to the political. I was able to draw on his generous help in yet another area, drawing on his expertise in Latin to translate source material when I revised my *True Adventures of Dr John Dee and Sir Edward Kelly*. Our meetings were regularly interrupted by people coming up to Father Stenhouse and greeting him with obvious affection and friendship, people old and young who knew him as priest and friend, many from overseas that he had helped when Catholic Chaplain to Asian students studying in Australian universities and schools. His generosity and sympathy and goodness were apparent in all these encounters, returning us from gloom about the world's political direction and western policies in the Middle East to the immediacy of caring human contact.

The world of writing, editing, contributing to newspapers and magazines, and talking to fellow writers and journalists was the world we had in common. Over the years he had numbered amongst his friends and associates such well known and diverse writers as Cyril Pearl, Alister Kershaw, Rupert Lockwood and more, and the columns of *Annals* demonstrate the range of the contributors he continued to recruit. During the war in Vietnam he ran two opposing pieces, one by David Armstrong the professor of philosophy advocating war, and one by David Armstrong of *The Australian* opposing it, happily exploiting the coincidence of names. He was never beyond a joke and delighted to publish the drawings and cartoons of Kevin Drumm.

But his was not a desk-bound life. His travels were wide and his experiences often startling. Like the time he was photographing some medieval building in the Bekaa valley and found himself surrounded by a posse of armed, mounted men who thought he was photographing their marijuana plantation. Or the time in Damascus when he inquired of the monastery cook what the evening meal consisted of and discovered that each night the cook went out and caught and cooked a stray cat. His energy and commitment were extraordinary. Right up until the end he was editing the 130th birthday issue of *Annals*, flying to Brisbane to give a paper on Islam and driving to Campion College to give a conference paper on John Farrell. While for his bedtime reading he was working through Grote's history of Ancient Greece. He was an inspiration.

Peerless And Fearless

Christopher Dawson

Newspaper offices, whether magnificent or insignificant, tend to have annexes — either a pub or a restaurant generally referred to as 'watering holes'.

It was in one such Sydney 'watering holes', the Italian restaurant, Alfredo's in Bulletin Place, that Father Paul Stenhouse and I had our last lunch together organised by the robust commentator, Piers Akerman. His opinions, it can be said, do not always fall within ABC parameters. We talked of friendships, Frank Devine and the food Father Paul enjoyed.

We were joined by Tony Abbott, whose copy I occasionally edited at *The Australian*, and talked about old times, but not his truncated career as Prime Minister in Canberra. We stressed how much we enjoyed Tony's friendship and admired his courage.

The occasion requires mention because it epitomised how Father Paul held the balance between journalism and religion. This he did as a member of vanishing species: the printer-journalist, able to write copy, edit it and set it. Mark Twain was a member of the species. So was Ken Cowley, co-founder of *The Australian* with Rupert Murdoch. Printer-journalists look on plain journalists with a benign but non-reverential eye. They listen and when they comment, it tends to be with a cutting edge. Maybe it was my name, Christopher Dawson, that first caught

Father Paul's attention. Scots-born and reared, I have Yorkshire antecedents, as did the great Catholic author; both our fathers were Lt. Colonels in the British Army and my father went to Dawson's old school, Winchester College. I shared a bank in Fleet Street—Childs—with the great Dawson and once found $400 pounds in my often rather empty account. I had to write from Cambridge that indeed they had found a historian but not the right one.

Regret is part of mourning and I'll always regret that Father Paul never came to Yorkshire; I could have shown him the Ridings and their ancient Catholic character — Ampleforth College, Whitby, Jervaulx and Fountains Abbeys even York Minster, that took 300 years to create to the glory of God; and much more. As it happens my Yorkshire inheritance has made me the Patron of the Living and Lay Rector of All Saints, Weston in Wharfedale. According to the Church of England the exercise of Patronage or Advowson is the right to present a priest to a particular benefice.

It is part of the historic, foundation element of the Church of England carried over from the pre-Reformation Church.

Today it apparently forms part of a system of checks and balances to ensure the continuance 'of a broad spectrum of belief and practice within the Church, not least traditional orthodoxy'.

Call me Ecumanist. I have appointed a friend and Roman Catholic as my proxy at All Saints, Weston. We have just chosen a new vicar, a former Army chaplain, once a Catholic, who conducted Anzac Day services for Australian troops in the Middle East.

Possibly Father Paul's views of these arcane arrangements

would have shown the cutting edge mentioned above.

All Saints, Weston itself would have been to his liking. It has a thousand years of Christianity, box pews, a Norman window, a three-decker pulpit, a Viking tombstone (in one hand of the Viking image is a sword, the other a woman) and a Tau Cross, a symbol of security in the Old Testament, adopted by the early Christians and later taken up by the Franciscan Order.

The Squire's Pew is the All Saints curiosity of curiosities. There the squire and his family could sit enclosed on comfortable chairs warmed by a small stove in the wall. I haven't used it much myself though its mine by inheritance from my father who died in 2011, aged 93 and, I like to think, rejoined the fallen of his regiment, the Queen's Own Cameron Highlanders.

A Very Special Friend

Giles Auty

The late Father Paul Stenhouse and I first met and began our long friendship at some time or other at the beginning of this century often in the company of notable former journalists the late Frank Devine and Paddy McGuinness. I believe I first wrote for *Annals* in fact in 2002 while working briefly for *The Courier Mail* in Brisbane. It all certainly seems quite a while ago.

So how and why did two people from opposite ends of our planet and radically different backgrounds form such a long, easy and rewarding friendship? The credit must surely go to Father Paul whose lengthy religious training probably helped give him an insight into the inner beings rather than just the superficial personalities of the rest of us.

Although we were much the same age our backgrounds could hardly have been more different. For example, in Father Paul's case his father died shortly before he was born. Although my father was a very distant figure at least I did have a father. Over time I came to think of my father in fact 'as the man at the bottom of our garden'—an impression prompted largely by his habit of retreating regularly with a portable table and a massive pile of reference books to the furthest extremity of our property. Towards the end of his scholarly career my late father Roland Ainsworth Auty became a principal reader for the *Complete Oxford English Dictionary*, contributing some 26,000 original entries to its 1970 *Supplement*.

Because my father barely acknowledged that children existed, no children's books graced our library shelves at home. One result of this was that I acquired a weirdly extended English vocabulary from a very early age to set beside the consequences of starting Latin at eight, French at nine and Ancient Greek at eleven. By a mere accident of birth in short I acquired the sort of education very few might even chance upon today. During my first year at an Anglican boarding school in another county I was deeply embarrassed in fact when an essay I had written on the subject of 'neighbours' was read out to the entire school. I think the word 'affability' appeared somewhere in my headline. I was just ten at the time.

Father Paul and the magazine he edited with so much flair for so many years came at last to parallel conclusions close to the end of 2019. In retrospect I suspect that Father Paul was politically somewhat to the Left of me which is hardly difficult since I am a staunchly conservative political, cultural and religious writer who possibly veers at times towards an extreme. But that is because I am passionately opposed to neo-Marxism which undermines democracy and proceeds largely by stealth. In an anthology of my essays published by Connor Court in 2016—*Culture at Crisis Point*—28 of the 50 essays were first published in *Annals*. My guess is that I probably wrote about 150 such in total. If I were ever late I was soon reminded of my unwritten obligation: ' For some strange reason my readers rather like your articles. Could you hurry along now with the next piece please...'

Yet strangely, as I recount clearly on the back cover of my anthology, my first intention in life was always to be a painter, a professional career I followed exclusively for about 25 years based largely at the extreme West of Cornwall which once boasted an international colony of artists of all kinds the like of which we may never see again. I began writing in fact in the studio I built in the roof of my house in Penzance which looked out onto the visual wonders of Mount's Bay.

The house was situated rather conveniently next door to the Catholic Church. Neither of my parents were churchgoers and I was received myself into the Catholic Church in 1962. A major influence was a first cousin, John Aquila Peace whose father was the last Minister of Labour in the final white Raj government in India. John, who was a formidable games player, was brought up partly by my parents in England before my sister and I were born. During the Second World War he was a much decorated war hero who fought through North Africa and Italy in charge of a body of men who hailed from India's then North West Frontier. In civil life he briefly became a lay brother at a Catholic monastery on the Isle of Wight. My own moment of receiving the gift of Faith involved a total review in my mind of the religious history of England. As a painter I had always loved our physical planet deeply and my conversion simply extended this love to a world of the spirit.

Within two years of my conversion to Rome, the opening salvo—political correctness—of postmodernism struck Europe and although its antecedents at first appeared to be American—a university in California—we now realise the concealed but virulently left-wing stance originated through a widespread acceptance of communist thinkers from Germany's pre-war Frankfurt School into American universities. Next came feminism and all the other 'isms' which were and are simply neo-Marxism in disguise. Part of my compulsory military service had been spent holding a front-line against Soviet forces in the frozen pine-woods of Northern Germany. Before communism's ostensible international collapse in 1989 both my future wife and I worked and travelled extensively in then communist countries: Latvia, East Germany, Poland, Slovakia, the Czech Republic, Georgia and the USSR itself. We certainly saw the horrors of communism at first hand for ourselves. Before coming to Australia I wrote a column broadly about art for the *The Spectator* in London for 11 years travelling overseas extensively in the years that I did so.

How many academics or others in Australia ever had genuine first-hand experience of communism for themselves? Karl Marx understood clearly that he could not establish his ideas totally without a final destruction of the family and Christianity. Sadly we draw closer to the latter twin events in Australia now every day.

Father Paul married my wife and me in a private chapel lent us kindly by Cardinal Pell in St.Mary's Cathedral, Sydney before his departure to Italy. I had worked previously for then Archbishop Pell advising him on improvements to St. Patrick's Cathedral in Melbourne such as the commissioning of the large bronze there of Archbishop Mannix. I had advised major clients for years on such matters before coming to Australia.

Father Paul's scholarly knowledge of the history of Islam set a world-class standard as his recent book on the subject abundantly proves. *Islam, Context and Complexity* (Australian Scholarly Publishing 2019) brings the present-day problems of multi-faith existence into sharp focus just as it does the true history of the beginnings of Islam. My scholarship on the subject of Marxism does not approach the standards set by Paul but I have travelled very extensively and observed closely and without bias to the best of my ability. Paul knew this and accepted much that I wrote on the subject with gratitude knowing it was written from an orthodox Catholic point of view. Today trade generally trumps politics in world economic terms but there is a very high price to be paid for this morally in the long run. Christianity and Catholicism in particular does not lend itself to deceitful selling which is the reverse side of post-modernism. I did not learn this overnight but have a very long span of adulthood to look back on. Paul visited us regularly in England where we lived for some years near Hampton Court. He often joined us on excursions into the ravishing countryside of Surrey and Sussex where we could introduce him to the very best England has to offer such as the village of Lodsworth in Sussex. This was the England many fought for so passionately during the Second World War—not so much for King and Country perhaps as King and Countryside. In Australia, Father Paul visited us very regularly at our home high in the Blue Mountains. Our dynasty of Airedale terriers Humphrey and Harry always knew he was coming from his telephone calls and greeted him with great enthusiasm. That said, even they could not possibly miss him more than we do.

Eight Men, Not One Man

R. J. Stove

'Roooooooooob!'. There could be no mistaking that unique light-baritone speaking voice which so often greeted me, when I answered a call from a Sydney number. That greeting was Fr Stenhouse's vocal signature, just as John Bercow's command in the House of Commons—'Or*derrrrrrrrrrrrr!*'— was *his* vocal signature. I now grieve at the realisation that never again in this life will that 'Rooooooooob!' float down the phone.

Considering that Fr Stenhouse and I (to me he was always 'Father' or 'Fr Stenhouse,' never 'Fr Paul', let alone 'Paul') wrote for several of the same late–1980s publications, I am surprised that our paths took so long to cross. That they did cross, I owe mostly to an expatriate friend we had in common: the late, great Alister Kershaw, whom during 1990 I met at his Loire Valley home. Alister lavished such hearty praise on Fr Stenhouse as to pique my interest, and I filed this enthusiasm in my memory-bank; but I somehow failed to meet Fr Stenhouse for another two years.

Over the next decade I turned into a regular *Annals* reader and then an occasional *Annals* writer, having already become an *Annals* recipient. (A useful research project for some bright graduate: to find a single Australian, living or dead, who actually paid full price for receiving *Annals* year after year. I know of no such Australian, though I know of several Australians—including non-Catholics—who were getting *Annals* gratis from the 1950s onwards.) That which Fr Stenhouse did very largely single-handed in keeping *Annals* going, would in the USA, France, or any Latin American country have required several dozen staffers.

On the extremely rare occasions when I had encountered an author whom even Fr Stenhouse had never heard of, I must admit to rather preening myself on this short-term, factitious attainment. Nineteen times out of 20, the intellectual debt operated in entirely the other direction: Fr Stenhouse had unearthed, for my and others' benefit, an obscure scribe from his prodigious library. How else but via *Annals* would I ever have stumbled across Christopher Hollis's *The American Heresy*? Or James Gairdner's accounts of the Lollards? Or Sir Arnold Lunn's rebuttal of H.C. Lea on the Spanish Inquisition? Or anything by Gabriel Marcel? Or anything by William Cobbett (perhaps Fr Stenhouse's greatest literary hero)? Or most of Chesterton? Or most of Belloc? Or most of Ronald Knox? The list could continue for pages.

Marking Fr Stenhouse's conversation—how desperately I miss our thrice-yearly late-breakfast get-togethers at Circular Quay—was a sportive delight in human foibles. During one such rendezvous, he suddenly admitted to never having mastered German. I replied that I found this failure hard to credit, given his extreme fluency in Arabic, Aramaic, and Hebrew as well as in the Romance languages. Yet still he insisted that German had always defeated him. As he explained the situation, though, it grew obvious that he found a certain philosophical merit in his linguistic shortcoming.

He embarked on the sad tale of a female student from his

Sydney University youth, circa 1959. This student one day alarmingly announced that she had begun studying German, so as to read Hegel in the original. On and on she toiled at her Teutonic grammatical apparatus; over and over she perused the *ipsissima verba* of Hegelian dialectic. In the end she reached (Fr Stenhouse sadly assured me) so esoteric a stage of enlightenment that she *had* to defend Hegel, through fear of being otherwise forced to admit that she would have remained happier for never having learnt a single German word. That notion she could not bear to contemplate. Prussian statist metaphysics trapped her as surely as regicide trapped Macbeth; and, like Macbeth, she had plunged 'in so far that should I wade no more / Returning were as tedious as go o'er.'

It was typical of Fr Stenhouse that my eventual submission to Rome (2002) did not make the slightest outward difference in our dealings. He knew where my religious loyalties lay, perhaps before I fully knew myself. Both before and after my conversion he displayed astounding financial generosity to me. When I once queried how *Annals* would survive if he showed (as he probably did show) similar financial generosity to other and more frequent *Annals* contributors, he calmly replied: '*Rerum Novarum* is still binding.'

I never presumed to ask Fr Stenhouse about the sexual abuse crisis which engulfed the Church during his last years. His innate cheerfulness of temperament and extreme busyness of schedule helped, I am convinced, to keep him from succumbing to despair.

Even more crucial to his endurance, I think, was that gift so rare among Australians as to seem almost weird: a gift for *institutional* loyalty. The commonest intellectual vice among

Australians is the precise opposite: an absurd over-confidence about achieving the political millennium through some individual or other. Fr Stenhouse allowed himself no such rash trust in merely secular messiahs. In the very marrow of his bones, he accepted the truth of Matthew 16:18. He thereby judged each passing doctrine—each political movement, each cultural vogue, each intellectual fad—according to its compatibility or incompatibility with the Catholic Church. On whose side, ultimately, was it? The side of Saints Thomas More, John Fisher, Edmund Campion, Margaret Clitherow, and Oliver Plunkett? Or the side of Henry VIII, Elizabeth I, William Cecil, Richard Topcliffe, and Titus Oates? Such clarity of mind, and the courage which it instils, Fr Stenhouse found to be as natural as breathing.

Meanwhile, the following passage from Sydney Smith (an *Annals* favourite) can stand as Fr Stenhouse's epitaph:

> The meaning of an extraordinary man is that he is eight men, not one man; that he has as much wit as if he had no sense, and as much sense as if he had no wit ... But when wit is combined with sense and information; when it is softened by benevolence and restrained by strong principle; when it is in the hands of a man who can use it and despise it, who can be witty, and something much better than witty, who loves honour, justice, decency, good-nature, morality, and religion ten thousand times better than wit; why, wit is then a beautiful part of our nature.

From the *Journal of the Australian Catholic Historical Society*

FROM CARDINAL GEORGE PELL

[George Pell's] deepest regret is the pain his ordeal caused his family and close friends. He was deeply saddened not to be able to visit Sydney priest Father Paul Stenhouse, the former editor of *Annals* magazine, when he was dying in November, after years of battling cancer. 'He was a dear friend and learned priest. We need more like him.'

'Diary of an Innocent Man', Tess Livingstone,
The Australian, Tuesday April 14 2020, Inquirer, p. 9

[At one time, Paul was asked by Cardinal Pell to be one his auxiliary bishops. Paul declined. He said he was not known by the Sydney clergy—but it would have been too restricting for the wide national and international ministry he was used to!]

The Contributors

Tony Abbott, journalist, politician, with some seminary experience, Prime Minister of Australia, 2013–2015.

Joseph Assaf. In 1967, at the age of 22, with no English, no money and no family, Joseph migrated to Australia from Lebanon in someone else's shoes. Upon arrival, he worked in a factory at night and studied during the day. In 1977 Joseph established Ethnic Communications, the world's first agency to specialize in multicultural marketing and later on, Multicall, the world's first multicultural call centre. Joseph has served as a member of many councils, boards and committees, In 1988, Joseph founded the Ethnic Business Awards, which celebrate the diversity and multiculturalism of Australia. In 2010 he created the Indigenous in Business award — a first of its kind. In June 2013, Joseph was appointed to the Civil Society 20 group — the C20 — as part of the wider engagement process for the G20 meeting in Australia in 2014. Joseph became a Member (AM) of the Order of Australia in the Queen's birthday 2010 honour list and then in 2014, he received the Lifetime Achievement Award from the Australian Migration and Settlement Council and in 2018, he was made an Officer of the Order of Australia (AO) for distinguished service to business and multiculturalism.

Giles Ainsworth Auty. Possibly the only Christian thing about my antecedents is my date of birth 1.11 1934 — All

Saints's Day—at Faversham in Kent. My father Roland
Ainsworth Auty was a notable scholar who worked on
revisions to the *Complete Oxford English Dictionary*. Like
my father I was educated as a boarder at Bancroft's School,
Woodford in England. My first ambition was to be a painter
and I subsequently became a journalist and author almost
by chance. I was received into the Catholic Church in 1962
largely through the influence of an older first cousin who
was a war hero: John Aquila Peace. I did military service
myself on the front-line against the USSR in Germany in
1954.

Anthony Brereton, Masters Teaching (Syd Uni), Secretary
NT Labor Party , former Teacher Catholic Education,Sydney,
Teacher NT Public School System, Darwin and Yirrkala.

Marek Jan Chodakiewicz, PhD, holds the Kosciuszko Chair
in Polish Studies and heads the Center for Intermarium
Studies at the Institute of World Politics: A Graduate School
of National Security and International Affairs, Washington,
DC.

Phillip John Collignon, born in Sydney to Dutch parents
who migrated to Australia in 1951. Educated at Marist
Brothers Parramatta and graduated with a BA Dip Educ.
from Macquarie University in 1978. Taught in State and
Catholics schools for 11 years. Australian National Director
of the international Catholic charity Aid to the Church in
Need 1990–2018. Now retired.

Christopher Dawson, ex-Harrow and Cambridge, ex-*Yorkshire Post*, ex-*Daily Express*, ex-*Sydney Morning Herald*, ex-*The Australian*, ex-Cameron Highlanders (TA), leader-writer and military historian.

Michael Fallon is a Missionary of the Sacred Heart (MSC). Since his ordination in 1961 his ministry has been largely devoted to teaching, ten years teaching in secondary schools, chaplain at the University of New South Wales, lectured at the then Saint Paul's National Seminary in Kensington NSW. From 1994 to 2001 he was in the parish of Henley Beach, Adelaide SA, since 2002 in the parish of Kippax, ACT. In 2014 he moved to Saint Mary's Towers, Douglas Park, as part of the Retreat House Team. He has published commentaries on all of the Books of the Old and New Testaments.

James Franklin is Honorary Professor in the School of Mathematics and Statistics, UNSW Sydney. His books include *Corrupting the Youth: A History of Philosophy in Australia* and *Catholic Values and Australian Realities*. He is editor of the *Journal of the Australian Catholic Historical Society*.

Dr, The Hon Tricia Kavanagh: Former Justice, NSW Industrial Court and Deputy President NSW Industrial Commission, Arbitrator International Court of Arbitration for Sport, Barrister-at-Law, former assistant to Fr Paul Stenhouse MSC, former Teacher.

James Littleton, Missionary of the Sacred Heart, professed in 1948, ordained 1955, his life ministry in MSC education, including Headmasters of MSC Colleges, Downlands

(Queensland), Chevalier (New South Wales), Daramalan (ACT). He served as Provincial Superior of the Missionaries of the Sacred Heart, 1987–92.

John Samuel Madden was born in Lithgow in 1950. He holds Bachelors' degrees in Arts and Law from the Australian National University and in Theology from the University of Newcastle. He is a retired lawyer having been engaged for 35 years in private practice, the Commonwealth Attorney-General's Department, the Federal Court of Australia and the Australian Government Solicitor.

Peter Macinante began work in the *Annals* Office in 1982 and continued through until the closure of *Annals*. He is archivist and librararian at Sacred Heart Monastery, Kensington.

Peter Malone, Missionary of the Sacred Heart, professed in 1958, ordained 1965. Has taught Old Testament Studies and Theology at the Yarra Theological Union, National Pastoral Institute, Heart of Life Centre. He edited Compass Theology Review, 1972–98. He reviewed films in Annals from 1968–98. From 1998–2005, he headed the Catholic Church's Media Organizations, OCIC and SIGNIS.

James Murray: Key education: St. Anthony's R.C. Infants School. Key text: *The Penny Catechism*. Key first movie: director Jim Cruse's *Covered Wagon*. James Murray's first and future wife, Jenny, keeps him in working order aided by their children and their children (at whose Catholic rites of passage Fr Paul Stenhouse—Editor-in-Excelsis!—presided).

Piers Paul Read, British novelist, historian and biographer.

In addition to his written works, Read is also a dramatist and television scriptwriter. In recent years, he has produced a number of authorized biographies and popular history books which are intended for a general audience.

Greg Quinn, Catholic, retired typesetter.

Robert James Stove, born in Sydney but based in Melbourne since 2001, is the author of *The Unsleeping Eye: Secret Police and Their Victims* (Encounter Books, New York, 2003) and of *César Franck: His Life and Times* (Scarecrow Press, Lanham, Maryland, 2012). He converted to Catholicism in 2002, and was a frequent contributor to *Annals*.

Karl Schmude has combined a career in university librarianship and freelance writing with a co-founder role in the development of Campion College Australia. He has published widely on religion and culture in Australian and international journals, including *Annals* for more than forty years, as well as producing short biographies of such authors as G.K. Chesterton, Hilaire Belloc, and Christopher Dawson.

Greg Sheridan, *The Australian*'s foreign editor, active across television and radio and also writes extensively on culture. He has written seven books. His latest, *God is Good for You: A Defence of Christianity in Troubled Times*, is a passionate defence of religious belief in a secular age. Before that, *When We Were Young and Foolish* was a memoir of culture, politics and journalism. As foreign editor, he specialises in Asia.

Wanda Skowronska is a Catholic psychologist and author living and working in Sydney. She completed a PhD. at the

John Paul II Institute in Melbourne in 2011 where she did sessional lecturing. Her most recent book is *Angels Incense and Revolution: Catholic Schooldays of the 1960s* (2019). She has written for several periodicals, including the Australian Catholic journal *Annals Australasia* for over 15 years.

Robert Teo. I was born in 1963 in a small town on the island of Borneo called Sibu. I am of Malaysian Chinese descent. Mid way through my high schooling in Malaysia, I decided it was only appropriate that I set foot to seek better opportunities to support both myself and my family. Migrating to Australia to complete the rest of my high schooling and as well as the university. I graduated from the University of New South Wales with an architectural bachelor's degree however funnily enough, to this day I have never practised as an architect. I decided to stay in Australia given the better opportunities and new standard of living. In 1990 I married to my beautiful wife Helen with the ceremony celebrated by Father Paul Stenhouse. We now have three boys aged 19, 23 and 26 and are very proud of them.

Michael Wilding is emeritus professor of English and Australian Literature at the University of Sydney. He is the author and editor of some 50 works of fiction, literary criticism, and documentary. Recent books include *Wild Bleak Bohemia: Marcus Clarke, Adam Lindsay Gordon and Henry Kendall: a Documentary*, the memoir *Growing Wild*, the collection of essays *Wild About Books* and the novels *Little Demon* and *The Travel Writer*.

Hendrikus Wong, born in Indonesia. His family migrated

to Australia in 1987 and lived permanently in Sydney since 1998. Converted to Catholicism in 1979 at the school run by the Daughters of Our Lady of the Sacred Heart. He obtained several University degrees. Worked for about 10 years for the MSC (*Annals* office and Mission Office), University of Notre Dame then to the private sector.

www.ingramcontent.com/pod-product-compliance
Ingram Content Group Australia Pty Ltd
76 Discovery Rd, Dandenong South VIC 3175, AU
AUHW020841060325
407965AU00004B/86